THE LADIES' GUIDE

to True Politeness and Perfect Manners

Eliza Leslie

THE LADIES' GUIDE TO TRUE POLITENESS AND
PERFECT MANNERS

First published by T. B. Peterson & Brothers in 1864
This revised edition published in 2016 by Summersdale Publishers Ltd
Images © Shutterstock or out of copyright

Summersdale Publishers Ltd
46 West Street
Chichester
West Sussex
PO19 1RP
UK

www.summersdale.com

Printed and bound in the Czech Republic

ISBN: 978-1-84953-828-2

Substantial discounts on bulk quantities of Summersdale books are available to corporations, professional associations and other organisations. For details contact Nicky Douglas by telephone: +44 (0) 1243 756902, fax: +44 (0) 1243 786300 or email: nicky@summersdale.com.

PREFACE

It is said that soon after the publication of *Nicholas Nickleby*, not fewer than six Yorkshire schoolmasters (or rather six principals of Yorkshire institutes) took journeys to London, with the express purpose of prosecuting Dickens for libels—"each one and severally" considering himself shown up to the world as Mr. Squeers of Dotheboys Hall.

Now, if Dickens had drawn as graphic a picture of Dothe*girls* Hall, we firmly believe that none of the lady principals of similar institutes would have committed themselves by evincing so little tact, and adopting such impolitic proceedings. They would wisely have held back from all appropriation of the obnoxious character, and passed it over unnoticed; as if it could not possibly have the slightest reference to *them*.

Therefore we wish that those of our fair readers whom certain hints in the following pages may awaken to the consciousness of a few habitual misbehavements, (of which they were not previously aware,) should pause, and reflect, before they allow themselves to "take umbrage too much." Let them keep in mind that the purpose of the writer is to amend, and not to offend; to improve her young countrywomen, and not to annoy them. It is with this view only that she has been induced to "set down in a note-book" such lapses from *les bienséances* as she has remarked during a long course of observation, and on a very diversified field.

She trusts that her readers will peruse this book in as friendly a spirit as it was written.

CONTENTS

Chapter I

SUGGESTIONS TO VISITERS

DEFINING YOUR STAY

An amusing writer of the last century, justly complains of the want of definite words to express, distinctly and unmistakably, the different degrees of visits, with reference to their length. Whether the stay of the guest comprises ten minutes, an hour, an evening, a day, a week, or a month, still it goes under the vague and general term of a visit.

We propose, humourously, that if the stay of the guest exceeds a week, it should be called "a visitation." If it includes dining, or tea-drinking, or evening-spending, it may be termed "a visit;" while a mere call can be mentioned as "a vis."

The idea is a very convenient one, and we should like to see it carried out by general adoption. Meanwhile, we must, for the present, be contented with the old uncertain practice of saying only "visit" and "visiter." We think it our duty to explain that this chapter is designed for the benefit of such inexperienced females as may be about to engage in what we should like to call "a visitation."

TO BEGIN AT THE BEGINNING

Do not *volunteer* a visit to a friend in the country, or in another town, unless you have had what is called "a standing invitation," with every reason to believe that it was sincerely and cordially given. Many invitations are mere "words of course," without meaning or motive, designed only to make a show of politeness, and not intended to be taken literally, or ever acted upon. Even when convinced that your friend is really your friend, that she truly loves you, has invited you in all sincerity, and will be happy in your society, still, it is best to apprise her, duly, of the exact day and hour when she may expect you; always with the proviso that it is convenient to herself to receive you at that time, and desiring her to let you know, candidly, if it is not. However close your intimacy, an unexpected arrival may possibly produce inconvenience to your hostess; particularly if her family is numerous, or her bedchambers few. The case is somewhat different, where the house is large, and where there is no scarcity of apartments for guests, of servants to wait on them, or of money to furnish the means of entertaining them liberally. But even then, the time of arrival should be previously intimated, and observed as punctually as possible. Such are now the facilities of travelling, and the rapidity of transmitting intelligence, that there is no excuse for unexpected or ill-timed visits; and when unexpected, they are too frequently ill-timed. When attempted as "agreeable surprises," they are seldom very agreeable to the surprised. Also the improvement in manners has rendered these incursions old-fashioned and ungenteel. Above all, never volunteer visits to families whose circumstances are so narrow that they can ill afford the expense of a guest.

RSVP PROMPTLY AND ACCORDINGLY

Having received an invitation, reply to it immediately; and do not keep your friends waiting, day after day, in uncertainty whether you mean to accept or decline it;

causing them, perhaps, to delay asking other visiters till they have ascertained if you are to be expected or not.

Excuse yourself from accepting invitations from persons whom you do not like, and whose dispositions, habits, feelings, and opinions are in most things the reverse of your own. There can be no pleasure in daily and familiar intercourse where there is no congeniality. Such visits never end well; and they sometimes produce irreconcilable quarrels, or at least a lasting and ill-concealed coolness. Though for years you may have always met on decent terms, you may become positive enemies from living a short time under the same roof; and there is something dishonourable in laying yourself under obligations and receiving civilities from persons whom you secretly dislike, and in whose society you can have little or no enjoyment.

OUTSTAYING YOUR WELCOME

When you arrive, take occasion to mention how long you intend to stay; that your hostess may plan her arrangements accordingly. It is rude and inconsiderate to keep her in ignorance of the probable duration of your visit. And when the allotted time has expired, do not be persuaded to extend it farther, unless you are earnestly, and with undoubted sincerity invited to do so. It is much better that your friends should part with you reluctantly, than you should give them reason to wish your visit shorter. Even if it *has* been very pleasant on both sides, it may not continue so if prolonged too far. Take care of wearing out your welcome. Besides, your room may be wanted for another guest.

ABIDE BY THE HOUSE RULES

On your first evening, enquire the hours of the house, that you may always be ready to comply with them. Rise early enough to be washed and dressed in time for breakfast; but if you are ready too early, remain in your own apartment, or walk about the garden, or go to the library till the cleaning and arranging of the sitting-room has been completed. Meanwhile, you can occupy yourself with a book, if you stay in your own room.

A TIP FROM THE AUTHOR

As soon as you quit your bed, take off the bedclothes, (each article separately,) and spread them widely over the chairs, turning the mattrass or bed as far down as it will go. This will give the bedding time to air; and in all houses it should be done every morning, the whole year round. Before you leave the room, raise the windows as high as they will go, (unless it should be raining, or snowing,) that the apartment may be well ventilated.

YOUR CHAMBERMAID'S CONDUCT

If when on a visit, you find that the chambermaid does not make your bed so that you can sleep comfortably, show her how to do it, (privately,) but say nothing to your hostess.

There is but one way of making a bed properly; and yet it is surprising how little that way is known or remembered. First, shake up the bed high and evenly; turning it over, and see that the foot is not higher than the head. If there is a mattrass above the bed, turn the mattrass half up, and then half down, till you have shaken up the bed beneath. Next spread on the under-sheet, laying it well over the bolster to secure it from dragging down and getting under the shoulders. However, to most beds now, there is a bolster-case. Then tuck in the under-sheet, well, at both sides, to prevent its getting loose and disordered in the night. For the same reason tuck in the upper-sheet, well, at the foot, leaving the sides loose. Tuck in the blankets at bottom, but not at the sides. Lay the counterpane smoothly over the whole. Turn it down at the top; and turn down the upper-sheet above it, so as to conceal the blankets entirely.

Should the chambermaid neglect your room, or be remiss in filling your pitchers, or in furnishing you with clean towels, speak to her on the subject when alone. She will hardly, for her own sake, inform her mistress that you have had occasion to find fault with her; unless she is very insolent or sulky, she will say she is sorry, and will promise to do better in future. Complaining to her mistress of these neglects will probably give offence to the lady, who may be of

12

that wayward (though too common) disposition which will allow no one except herself, to find any deficiency in *her* servants. As mistresses are frequently very touchy on these points, your hostess may hint that your statement is incredible, and that "no one ever complained before." Above all things, avoid letting her know that you have found or felt insects in your bed; a circumstance that may chance sometimes to happen even in the best kept houses. In a warm climate, or in an old house, the utmost care and the most vigilant neatness cannot always prevent it. It may be caused by the bringing of baggage from boats, or ships, and by servants neglecting their own beds; a too common practice with them, unless the mistress or her housekeeper compels them to be cleanly, and sees that they are so.

If you have proof positive that your bed is not free from these intolerable nuisances, confide this fact to the chambermaid only, and desire her to attend to it speedily. She will do so the more readily, if you promise her a reward in case of complete success. Enjoining her to manage this as quietly as possible, and to say nothing about it to any one, may spare you a scene with your hostess; who, though you have always regarded her as your warm friend, may, notwithstanding, become your enemy for life, in consequence of your having presumed to be incommoded in *her* house, where "nobody ever complained before." A well-bred, sensible, good-tempered woman will not, of course, take offence for such a cause; and will believe that there must have been good reason for the complaint, rather than suppose that her guest and her friend would mention so delicate a subject even to a servant, unless there was positive proof. And she will rightly think it was well to make it known, and have it immediately remedied. But all women who invite friends to visit them, are not sensible and good-tempered. Therefore, take care.

For similar reasons, should a servant purloin any article belonging to you, (and servants, considered quite honest, will sometimes pilfer from a visiter when they would not dare to do so from their mistress,) it is safest to pass it over, unless the article stolen is of consequence. You may find your hostess very unwilling to believe that a servant of *hers* could possibly be dishonest; and much may be said, or evidently *thought*, that will be very painful to you, her guest.

AVOID PUTTING UNDUE STRESS UPON YOUR HOSTESS

Notwithstanding all that may be said to you about "feeling yourself perfectly at home," and "considering your friend's house as your own," be very careful not literally to do so. In fact, it is impossible you *should* with any propriety—particularly, if it is your first visit. You cannot possibly know the real character and disposition of any acquaintance, till after you have had some experience in living under the same roof. If you find your hostess all that you can desire, and that she is making your visit every way agreeable, be very grateful to her, and let her understand that you are exceedingly happy at her house; but avoid staying too long, or taxing her kindness too highly.

Avoid encroaching unreasonably upon her time. Expect her not to devote an undue portion of it to you.

She will probably be engaged in the superintendence of household affairs, or in the care of her young children, for two or three hours after breakfast. So at these hours do not intrude upon her,—but amuse yourself with some occupation of your own, till you see that it is convenient to the family for you to join them in the sitting-room. In summer afternoons, retire for an hour or more, soon after dinner, to your own apartment, that you may give your friends an opportunity of taking their naps, and that you may do the same yourself. You will be brighter in the evening, from indulging in this practice; and less likely to feel sleepy, when you ought to be wide awake, and ready to assist in entertaining your entertainers. A silent visiter, whether silent from dulness or indolence, or a habit of taciturnity, is never an agreeable one.

Yet, however pleasant the conversation, have sufficient self-denial to break off in seasonable time, so as not to keep the family up by continuing in the parlour till a late hour. Some of them may be tired and sleepy, though you are not. And between ten and eleven o'clock it is well to retire.

YOUR CONDUCT AS GUEST

If you have shopping to do, and are acquainted with the town, you can be under no necessity of imposing on any lady of the family the task of accompanying you. To shop *for* others, or *with* others, is a most irksome fatigue. Even when a stranger in the place, you can easily, by enquiring of the family, learn where the best stores are to be found, and go to them by yourself.

While you are a guest at the house of a friend, do not pass too much of your time in visiting at *other* houses, unless she is with you. You have no right to avail yourself of the conveniences of eating and sleeping at her mansion, without giving her and her family the largest portion of your company.

While a guest yourself, it is taking an unwarrantable liberty to invite any of your friends or relatives to come there and spend a day or days.[1]

Refrain from visiting any person with whom your hostess is at enmity, even if that person has been one of your own intimate friends. You will in all probability be regarded as "a spy in the camp." There is nothing so difficult as to observe a strict neutrality; and on hearing both sides, it is scarcely possible not to lean more to the one than to the other. The friend whose hospitality you are enjoying will soon begin to look coldly upon you, if she finds you seeking the society of her enemy; and she may evince that coldness whenever you come home from these visits. However unjust her suspicions, it is too probable she may begin to think that you are drawn in to make her, and her house, and family, subjects of conversation when visiting her adversary; therefore, she will cease to feel kindly toward you. If you understand, soon after your arrival, that there is no probability of a reconciliation, send at once a concise note to the lady with whom your hostess is at variance; express your regret at the circumstance, and excuse yourself from visiting her while you remain in your present residence. This note should

---

[1] So it is to order the carriage without first asking permission of your hostess.

be polite, short, and decisive, and so worded as to give no offence to either side; for, before sending, it is proper for you to show it, while yet unsealed, to the friend with whom you are staying. And then let the correspondence be carried no further. The lady to whom it is addressed, will, of course, return a polite answer; such as you may show to your hostess.

It is to be presumed, she will not be so lost to all delicacy and propriety, as to intrude herself into the house of her enemy for the purpose of visiting you. But, if she does, it is your place civilly to decline seeing her. A slight coolness, a mere offence on a point of etiquette, which, if let alone, would die out like a tinder-spark, has been fanned, and blown into a flame by the go-betweening of a so-called *mutual friend*. We repeat, while you are a visiter at a house, hold no intercourse with any foe of that house. It is unkind and disrespectful to the family with whom you are staying, and very unsafe for yourself.

A TIP FROM THE AUTHOR

If you know that your friends are hurried with their sewing, or with preparations for company, offer to assist them, as far as you can. But if you are conscious of an incapacity to do such things well, it is better to excuse yourself by candidly saying so, than to attempt them and spoil them. At the same time, express your willingness to learn, if permitted. And you may learn, while staying at the house of a clever, notable friend, many things that you have hitherto had no opportunity of acquiring.

YOUR VISITER'S CONDUCT

When called on by any of your own acquaintances, they will not expect you to ask them to stay to tea, or to dinner. That is the business of your hostess—not yours.

If you are a young lady that has beaux, remember that you have no right to encourage the over-frequency of their visits in any house that is not your home, or to devote much of your time and attention to flirtation with them. Above all, avoid introducing to the family of your entertainers, young men whom they are likely in any respect to disapprove. No stranger who has the feelings of a gentleman, will make a *second* visit to any house unless he is invited by the head of the family, and he will take care that his visits shall not begin too early, or continue too late. However delightful he may find the society of his lady-fair, he has no right to incommode the family with whom she is staying, by prolonging his visits to an unseasonable hour. If he seems inclined to do so, there is nothing amiss in his fair-one herself hinting to him that it is past ten o'clock. Also, there should be "a temperance" even in his morning calls. It is rude in a young lady and gentleman to monopolise one of the parlours nearly all the forenoon—even if they are *really* courting—still more if they are only pretending to court; for instance, sitting close to each other, and whispering on subjects that might be discussed aloud before the whole house, and talked of across the room.

Young ladies noted for abounding in beaux, are generally rather inconvenient visiters; except in very spacious houses, and in gay, idle families. They should not take the liberty of inviting the said beaux to stay to dinner or to tea. Leave that civility to the head of the house,—without whose invitation no *gentleman* ought to remain.

LUGGAGE REQUIREMENTS

It is proper for visiters to put out and pay for their own washing, ironing, &c. Therefore, carry among your baggage two clothes-bags; one to be taken away by the laundress, the other to receive your clothes in the interval. You may always hear of a washerwoman, by enquiring of the servants of the house.

Take with you a small writing-case, containing whatever stationery you may be likely to want during your visit; including post-office stamps. Thus you will spare yourself, and spare the family, the inconvenience of applying to them whenever you have occasion for pen, ink, paper, &c. If you have no ink with you, the first time you go out, stop in at a stationer's store, and buy a small sixpenny bottle that will stand steadily alone, and answer the purpose of an inkstand. Also, take care to be well supplied with all sorts of sewing articles. There are young ladies who go from home on long visits, quite unprovided with even thimbles and scissors; depending all the time on borrowing. Many visiters, though very agreeable in great things, are exceedingly troublesome in little ones.

Take care not to slop your washing-stand, or to lay a piece of wet soap upon it. Spread your wet towels carefully on the towel-rail. See that your trunks are not placed so near the wall as to injure the paper or paint when the lid is thrown back.

If, when travelling, you are to stop but one night at the house of a friend, it is not necessary, for that one night, to have *all* your baggage carried up-stairs, particularly if your trunks are large or heavy. Before leaving home, put into your carpet-bag all the things you will require for that night; and then no other article of your baggage need be taken up to your chamber. They can be left down-stairs, in some safe and convenient place, which your hostess will designate. This will save much trouble, and preclude all the injury that may otherwise accrue to the banisters and staircase-wall, by the corners of trunks knocking against them. It is possible to put into a carpet-satchel (that can be carried in your own hand) a night-gown and night-cap, (tightly rolled,) with hair-brush, combs, tooth-brush, &c. It is surprising how much these hand-satchels may be made to contain, when packed closely. No lady or gentleman should travel without one. In going from home for one night only, a satchel is, frequently, all that is requisite.

ON YOUR DEPARTURE

On concluding your visit, tell your entertainers that it has been pleasant, and express your gratitude for the kindness you have received from them, and your hope that they will give you an opportunity of returning their civilities. Give a parting gratuity to each of the servants—the sum being according to your means, and to the length of your visit.

After you get home, write very soon (within two or three days) to the friend at whose house you have been staying, tell her of your journey, &c., and allude to your visit as having been very agreeable.

The visit over, be of all things careful not to repeat any thing that has come to your knowledge in consequence, and which your entertainers would wish to remain unknown. While inmates of their house, you may have unavoidably become acquainted with some particulars of their way of living not generally known, and which, perhaps, would not raise them in public estimation, if disclosed. Having been their guest, and partaken of their hospitality, you are bound in honour to keep silent on every topic that would injure them in the smallest degree, if repeated. Unhappily, there are ladies so lost to shame, as, after making a long visit, to retail for the amusement of their cronies, all sorts of invidious anecdotes concerning the family at whose house they have been staying; adding by way of corroboration—"I assure you this is all true, for I stayed five or six weeks at their house, and had a good chance of knowing." More shame then to tell it!

Whatever painful discoveries are made during a visit, should be kept as closely secret as if secrecy was enjoined by oath. It is not sufficient to refrain from "mentioning names." No clue should be given that could possibly enable the hearers even to hazard a guess.

Chapter II

THE VISITED

BEFORE YOUR GUEST ARRIVES

Having invited a friend to pass a few days or weeks at your house, and expecting her at a certain time, send a carriage to meet her at the rail-road depôt or the steamboat wharf, and if her host or hostess goes in it, so much the better; but do not take the children along, crowding the vehicle, for the sake of giving them a ride. Arriving at your house, have her baggage taken at once to the apartment prepared for her, and when she goes up-stairs, send a servant with her to unstrap her trunks. Then let her be left *alone* to arrange her dress. It is to be supposed that before her arrival, the mistress of the house has inspected the chamber of her guest, to see that all is right—that there are *two* pitchers full of fresh water on the stand, and three towels on the rail, (two fine and one coarse,) with a china mug for teeth-cleaning, and a tumbler to drink from; a slop jar of course, and a foot-bath. We conclude that in all genteel and well-furnished houses, none of these articles are wanting in every bedroom. On the mantel-piece a candle or lamp, with a box of lucifer matches beside it—the candle to be replaced by a new one every morning when the chambermaid arranges the room—or the lamp to be trimmed daily; so that the visiter may have a light at hand whenever she pleases, without ringing the bell and waiting till a servant brings one up.

By-the-bye, when a guest is expected, see previously that the bells and locks of her room are in order; and if they are not, have them repaired.

If it is cold weather, let her find a good fire in her room; and the shutters open, that she may have sufficient light. Also an extra blanket, folded, and laid on the foot of the bed. If summer, let the sashes be raised, and the shutters bowed. The room should have an easy chair with a heavy foot-cushion before it,—a low chair also, to sit on when shoes and stockings are to be changed, and feet washed. In a spare chamber there should be both a mattrass and a feather-bed, that your visiters may choose which they will have uppermost. Though you and all your own family may like to sleep hard, your guests may find it difficult to sleep at all on a mattrass with a paillasse under it. To many constitutions hard sleeping is not only intolerable, but pernicious to health.

Let the centre-table be furnished with a writing-case well supplied with all that is necessary, the inkstand filled, and with *good black ink*; and some sheets of letter-paper and note-paper laid near it. Also, some books, such as you think your friend will like. Let her find, at least, one bureau vacant; *all* the drawers empty, so that she may be able to unpack her muslins, &c., and arrange them at once. The same with the wardrobe or commode, so that she may have space to hang up her dresses—the press-closet, likewise, should be for her use while she stays.

By giving up the spare bedroom *entirely* to your visiter you will very much oblige her, and preclude the necessity of disturbing or interrupting her by coming in to get something out of drawers, closets, &c.

ACCOMMODATING YOUR GUEST

Every morning, after the chambermaid has done her duty, (the room of the visiter is the first to be put in order,) the hostess should go in to see that all is right. This done, no further inspection is necessary for that day.

It is not pleasant to be a guest in a house where you perceive that your hostess is continually and fretfully on the watch, lest some almost imperceptible injury should accrue to the furniture. We have known ladies who were always uneasy when their visiters sat down on a sofa or an ottoman, and could not forbear inviting them to change their seats and take chairs. We suppose the fear was that the more the damask-covered seats were used, the sooner they would wear out.

It is very kind and considerate to enquire of your guest if there is any dish, or article of food that she particularly likes, so that you may have it on the table while she stays; and also, if there is any thing peculiarly disagreeable to her, so that you may refrain from having it during her visit. A well-bred and sensible woman will not encroach upon your kindness, or take an undue advantage of it, in this respect or any other.

For such deficiencies as may be avoided or remedied, refrain from making the foolish apology that you consider her "no stranger"—and that you regard her "just as one of the family." If you invite her at all, it is your duty, for your own sake as well as hers, to treat her well in every thing. You will lose nothing by doing so.

If she desires to assist you in sewing, and has brought no work of her own, you may avail yourself of her offer, and employ her in moderation—but let it be in moderation only, and when sitting in the family circle. When alone in her own room, she, of course, would much rather read, write, or occupy herself in some way for her own benefit, or amusement. There are ladies who seem to expect that their guests should perform as much work as hired seamstresses.

Let the children be strictly forbidden to run into the apartments of visiters. Interdict them from going thither, unless sent with a message; and then let them be made to understand that they are always to knock at the door, and not go in till desired to do so. Also, that they are not to play and make a noise in the neighbourhood of her room. And when she comes into the parlour, that they are not to jump on her lap, put their hands into her pockets, or rummage her work-basket, or rumple and soil her dress by clinging to it with their hands. Neither should they be permitted to amuse themselves by rattling on the lower keys when she is playing on the piano, or interrupt her by teasing her all the time to play "for them to dance." All this we have seen, and the mothers have never checked it. To permit children to ask visiters for pennies or sixpences is mean and contemptible. And, if money *is* given them by a guest, they should be made to return it immediately.

Enquire on the first evening, if your visiter is accustomed to taking any refreshment before she retires for the night. If she is, have something sent up to her room every night, unless your own family are in the same habit. Then let sufficient for all be brought into the parlour. These little repasts are very pleasant, especially at the close of a long winter evening, and after coming home from a place of public amusement.

ON YOUR GUEST'S DEPARTURE

To "welcome the coming— speed the parting guest"— is a good maxim. So when your visiter is about to leave you, make all smooth and convenient for her departure. Let her be called up at an early hour, if she is to set out in the morning. Send a servant up to strap and bring down her trunks, as soon as she has announced that they are ready; and see that an early breakfast is prepared for her, and some of the family up and dressed to share it with her. Slip some cakes into her satchel for her to eat on the road, in case, by some chance, she should not reach the end of her journey at the usual hour. Have a carriage at the door in due time, and let some male member of the family accompany her to the starting-place and see her off, attending to her baggage and procuring her tickets.

Chapter III

TEA VISITERS

WELCOMING YOUR GUEST

When you have invited a friend to take tea with you, endeavour to render her visit as agreeable as you can; and try by all means *to make her comfortable*.

The domestic that attends the door should be instructed to show the guest up-stairs, as soon as she arrives; conducting her to an unoccupied apartment, where she may take off her bonnet, and arrange her hair, or any part of her dress that may require change or improvement. The lady should then be left to herself. Nothing is polite that can possibly incommode or embarrass—therefore, it is a mistaken civility for the hostess, or some female member of the family to follow the visiter up-stairs, and remain with her all the time she is preparing for her appearance in the parlour. We have seen an inquisitive little girl permitted by her mother to accompany a guest to the dressing-table, and watch her all the while she was at the glass; even following her to the corner in which she changed her shoes; the child talking, and asking questions incessantly. This should not be. Let both mothers and children understand that, on all occasions, over-officiousness is not politeness, and that nothing troublesome and inconvenient is ever agreeable.

FRESHENING UP

The toilet-table should be always furnished with a clean hair-brush, and a nice comb. We recommend those hair-brushes that have a mirror on the back, so as to afford the lady a glimpse of the back of her head and neck. Better still, as an appendage to a dressing-table, is a regular hand-mirror, of sufficient size to allow a really *satisfactory* view. These hand-mirrors are very convenient, to be used in conjunction with the large dressing-glass. Their cost is but trifling. The toilet-pincushion should always have pins in it. A small work-box properly furnished with needles, scissors, thimble, and cotton-spools, ought also to find a place on the dressing-table, in case the visiter may have occasion to repair any accident that may have happened to her dress.

A TIP FROM THE AUTHOR

For want of proper attention to such things, in an ill-ordered, though perhaps a very showy establishment, we have known an *expected* visiter ushered first into a dark entry, then shown into a dark parlour with an ashy hearth, and the fire nearly out: then, after groping her way to a seat, obliged to wait till a small hand-lamp could be procured to light her dimly up a steep, sharp-turning stair-case; and then, by the same lamp, finding on the neglected dressing-table a broken comb, an old brush, and an empty pincushion,—or (quite as probably) nothing at all—not to mention two or three children coming to watch and stare at her. On returning to the parlour, the visiter would probably find the fire just then making up, and the lamp still unlighted, because it had first to be trimmed. Meanwhile, the guest commences her visit with an uncomfortable feeling of self-reproach for coming too early; all things denoting that she was not expected so soon. In such houses everybody comes too early. However late, there will be nothing in readiness.

SEATING ARRANGEMENTS

The hostess should be in the parlour, prepared to receive her visiter, and to give her at once a seat in the corner of a sofa, or in a fauteuil, or large comfortable chair; if a rocking-chair, a footstool is an indispensable appendage. By-the-bye, the dizzy and ungraceful practice of rocking in a rocking-chair is now discontinued by all genteel people, except when entirely alone. A lady should never be seen to rock in a chair, and the rocking of a gentleman looks silly. Rocking is only fit for a nurse putting a baby to sleep. When children get into a large rocking-chair, they usually rock it over backward, and fall out. These chairs are now seldom seen in a parlour. Handsome, stuffed easy chairs, that are moved on castors, are substituted—and of these, half a dozen of various forms are not considered too many.

A COMFORTABLE TEMPERATURE

Give your visiter a fan to cool herself, if the room is warm, or to shade her eyes from the glare of the fire or the light—for the latter purpose, a broad hand-screen is generally used, but a palm-leaf fan will do for both. In buying these fans, choose those whose handle is the firm natural stem, left remaining on the leaf. They are far better than those with handles of bamboo, which in a short time become loose and rickety.

There are many persons who, professing never to use a fan themselves, seem to think that nobody can by any chance require one; and therefore they selfishly keep nothing of the sort in their rooms.

THE RIGHT TIME AND THE RIGHT PLACE

If, in consequence of dining very late, you are in the custom of also taking tea at a late hour—or making but slight preparations for that repast—waive that custom when you expect a friend whom you know to be in the practice of dining early, and who, perhaps, has walked far enough to feel fatigued, and to acquire an appetite. For her accommodation, order the tea earlier than usual, and let it be what is called "a *good* tea." If there is ample room at table, do not have the tea carried round,—particularly if you have but one servant to hand the whole. It is tedious, inconvenient, and unsatisfactory. There is no comfortable way of eating bread and butter, toast, or buttered cakes, except when seated at table. When handed round, there is always a risk of their greasing the dresses of the ladies— the greasing of fingers is inevitable—though that is of less consequence, now that the absurd practice of eating in gloves is wisely abolished among genteel people.

Still, if the company is too numerous for all to be commodiously seated at the usual family table, and if the table cannot be enlarged—it is better to have tea carried round by *two* servants, even if an extra one is hired for the occasion, than to crowd your guests uncomfortably. One person too many will cause inconvenience to all the rest, however the hostess may try to pass it off, by assuring the company that there is quite room enough, and that she has seen a still larger number seated round that very table. Everybody knows that "what's impossible a'n't true."

PREPARATIONS

In setting a tea-table, see that there is not only enough, but *more than enough* of cups and saucers, plates, knives and forks, spoons, napkins, &c. Let the *extra* articles be placed near the lady of the house,—to be distributed, if wanted. We have known families who had the means and the inclination to be hospitable, that never sat down to table without several spare *covers*, as the French call them, ready for accidental guests.

Unless you have domestics on whom you can implicitly rely, it is well to go into the eating-room about ten minutes before the announcement of tea, and to see that all is right; that the tea is strong and properly made, and the pot (which should be scalded twice) is not filled nearly to overflowing with a superabundance of water. The practice of drowning away all the flavour of the tea is strangely prevalent with servants; who are also very apt to neglect scalding the tea-pot; and who do not, or will not, remember that the kettle should be boiling hard at the moment the water is poured on the tea—otherwise the infusion will be insipid and tasteless, no matter how liberally the Chinese plant has been afforded.

If your cook is not *habitually* a good coffee-maker, the coffee will most probably be sent in cold, thick, and weak—for want of some previous supervision. Let it have that supervision.

We have heard of tea-tables (even in splendid establishments) being left entirely to the *mis*management of incompetent or negligent servants; so that when the company sat down, there was found a deficiency in some of the indispensable appendages; such as spoons, and even forks, and napkins—butter-knives forgotten, and (worse than all) *cooking-butter* served in mistake for the better sort. By-the-bye, the use of cooking-butter should be abolished in all genteel-houses. If the butter is not good enough to eat on the surface of cold bread or on warm cakes, it is not good enough to eat in the inside of sweet cakes, or in pastry, or in any thing else; and is totally unfit to be mixed with vegetables or sauces. The use of butter is to make things taste well; if it makes them taste ill, let it be entirely omitted: for bad butter is not only unpalatable, but unwholesome. There are houses in which the money wasted on one useless bauble for the drawing-room would furnish the family with excellent fresh butter for a whole year— enough for all purposes.

If cakes for tea have been made at home, and they have turned out failures, (as is often the case with home-made cakes where there is not much practice in baking them,) do not have them brought to table at all, but send to a shop and get others. It is rude to set before your guests what you know is unfit for them to eat. And heavy, tough, ill-baked things are discreditable to any house where the means of obtaining better are practicable.

In sending for cakes to a confectioner, do not *a second time* allow him to put you off with stale ones. This many confectioners are in the practice of doing, if it is passed over without notice. Stale cakes should at once be sent back, (with a proper reproof,) and fresh ones required. Let the confectioner with whom you deal understand that he is *not* to palm off his stale cakes upon *you*, and that you will not keep them when sent. You will then find that fresh ones will generally be forthcoming. It is always well to send for cakes in the early part of the afternoon.

Have a pitcher of ice-water on the side-table, and a tumbler beside every plate—as most persons like to finish with a glass of water.

A PROPER FAREWELL

If you invite a friend to tea, in whose own family there is no gentlemen, or no man-servant, it is your duty previously to ascertain that you can provide her on that evening with an escort home; and in giving the invitation, you should tell her so, that she may know on what to depend. If you keep a carriage, it will be most kind to send her home in it.

Even if it is your rule to have the entry-lamp extinguished at a certain hour, let your servants understand that this rule must be dispensed with, as long as an evening-visiter remains in the house. Also, do not have the linen covers put on the furniture, and the house audibly shut up for the night, before she has gone. To do this is rude, because she cannot but receive it as a hint that she has staid too long.

If your visiter is obliged to go home with no other escort than your servant-man, apprise him, in time, that this duty will be expected of him; desiring that he takes care to be at hand before ten o'clock.

A TIP FROM THE AUTHOR

A lady that has no escort whose services she can command, ought not to make unexpected tea-visits. In many cases these visits produce more inconvenience than pleasure. If you wish to "take tea sociably" with a friend, inform her previously of your intention. She will then let you know if she is disengaged on that evening, or if it is in any way inconvenient to receive you; and she will herself appoint another time. Generally, it is best not to volunteer a tea-visit, but to wait till invited.

STANDARDS OF DOUBLE-BOOKING

If you are engaged to take tea with an intimate friend, who assures you that you will see none but the family; and you afterward receive an invitation to join a party to a place of public amusement, which you have long been desirous of visiting, you may retract your first engagement, provided you send an apology in due time, telling the exact truth, and telling it in polite terms. Your intimate friend will then take no offence, considering it perfectly natural that you should prefer the concert, the play, or the exhibition, to a quiet evening passed at her house with no other guests. But take care to let her know as early as possible.[2] And be careful not to disappoint her again in a similar manner.

A SOCIABLE OCCASION

In inviting "a few friends," which means a small select company, endeavour to assort them suitably, so as not to bring together people who have no community of tastes, feelings, and ideas. If you mix the dull and stupid with the bright and animated, the cold and formal with the frank and lively, the professedly serious with the gay and cheerful, the light with the heavy, and above all, those who pride themselves on high birth with those who boast of "belonging to the people," none of these "few friends" will enjoy each other's society; the evening will *not* go off agreeably, and you and the other members of your family will have the worst of it. The pleasantest people in the room will naturally congregate together, and the task of entertaining the unentertainable will devolve on yourself and your own people.

Still, it is difficult always to assort your company to your satisfaction and theirs. A very charming lady may have very dull or very silly sisters. An intelligent and refined daughter may be unfortunate in a coarse, ignorant mother, or a prosing, tiresome, purse-proud father.

---

[2] Where the city-post is to be depended on, a note can always be sent in that way.

TO RETURN TO THE TEA-TABLE

Unless you are positively sure, when you have a visiter, that she drinks the same tea that is used in your own family, you should have both black and green on the table. Either sort is often extremely disagreeable to persons who take the other. Drinkers of green tea, for instance, have generally an unconquerable aversion to black, as tasting like hay, herbs, &c., and they find in it no refreshing or exhilarating property. In some, it produces nausea. Few, on the other hand, dislike the taste of *good* green tea, but they assign as a reason for not drinking it, that it is supposed from its enlivening qualities to affect the nerves. Judge Bushrod Washington, who always drank green, and avoided black, said that, "he took tea as a beverage, not as a medicine." And there are a vast number of sensible people in the same category. If your guest is a votary of green tea, have it made for her, in time for the essence of the leaves to be well drawn forth. It is no compliment to give her green tea that is weak and washy. And do not, at your own table, be so rude as to lecture her upon the superior wholesomeness of black tea. For more than a century, green tea was universally drunk in every house, and there was then less talk of nervous diseases than during the reign of Souchong,—which, by-the-bye, is nearly exploded in the best European society.

In pouring out, do not fill the cups to the brim. Always send the cream and sugar round, that each person may use those articles according to their own taste. Also, send round a small pot of hot water, that those who like their tea weak may conveniently dilute it.

A TIP FROM THE AUTHOR

Whether at dinner or tea, if yourself and family are in the habit of eating fast, (which, by the way, is a very bad and unwholesome one, and justly cited against us by our English cousins,) and you see that your visiter takes her food deliberately, endeavour (for that time at least) to check the rapidity of your own mastication, so as not to finish before she has done, and thus compel her to hurry herself uncomfortably, or be left alone while every one round her is sitting unoccupied and impatient. Or rather, let the family eat a little more than usual, or seem to do so, out of politeness to their guest.

When refreshments are brought in after tea, let them be placed on the centre-table, and handed round from thence by the gentlemen to the ladies. If there are only four or five persons present, it may be more convenient for all to sit round the table—which should not be cleared till after all the visiters have gone, that the things may again be offered before the departure of the guests.

A SURPRISE VISIT

Should chance-visiters come in before the family have gone to tea, let them at once be invited to partake of that repast; which they will of course decline, if they have had tea already. In a well-provided house, there can be no difficulty in adding something to the family tea-table, which, in genteel life, should never be discreditably parsimonious.

It is a very mean practice, for the members of the family to slip out of the parlour, one by one at a time, and steal away into the eating-room, to avoid inviting their visiter to accompany them. The truth is always suspected by these separate exits, and the length of absence from the parlour—and is frequently betrayed by the rattle of china, and the pervading fumes of hot cakes. How much better to meet the inconvenience (and it cannot be a great one) by decently conducting your accidental guest to the table, unless he says he has already taken tea, and will amuse himself with a book while the family are at theirs.

A TIRESOME CROWD

Casual evening visiters should avoid staying too late. Ten o'clock, in our country, is the usual time to depart, or at least to begin departing. If the visit is unduly prolonged, there may be evident signs of irrepressible drowsiness in the heads of the family, which, when perceived, will annoy the guest, who must then feel that he has stayed too long—and without being able to excuse himself with any approach to the elegance of William Spencer's apology to the charming Lady Anne Hamilton.

Too late I stay'd—forgive the crime; Unheeded flew the hours, For noiseless falls the foot of Time That only treads on flowers. Ah! who with clear account remarks The ebbing of the glass, When all its sands are diamond sparks, That dazzle as they pass!

Chapter IV

INTRODUCTIONS

THE IMPORTANCE OF INTRODUCTIONS

Fashion, in its various unmeaning freaks, sometimes decrees that it is not "stylish to introduce strangers." But this is a whim that, whenever attempted, has neither become general nor lasted long. It has seldom been adopted by persons of good sense and good manners—and very rarely by that fortunate class whose elevated standing in society enables them to act as they please, in throwing aside the fetters of absurd conventionalities, and who can afford to do so.

Non-introduction has been found, in many instances, to produce both inconvenience and vexation. Persons who had long known each other by reputation, and who would have rejoiced in an opportunity of becoming personally acquainted, have met in society, without being aware of it till afterward; and the opportunity has never recurred. One of our most distinguished literary Americans was seated at a dinner-party next to an European lady equally distinguished in literature; but as there were no introductions, he was not aware of her presence till the party was over and the lady gone. The lady knew who the gentleman was, and would gladly have conversed with him; but as he did not speak, because he was not introduced, she had not courage to commence—though she might have done so with perfect propriety, considering who *he* was, and who *she* was.

Still worse—from not knowing who are present, you may inadvertently fall upon a subject of conversation that, for private reasons, may be extremely irksome or painful to some of the company; for instance, in discussing a public character. Severe or mortifying remarks may unintentionally be made on the near relative, or on the intimate companion, of one whom you would on no account desire to offend. And in this way you may make enemies, where, under other circumstances, you would have made friends. In such cases, it is the duty of the hostess, or of any mutual acquaintance, immediately to introduce both parties, and thus prevent any further animadversions that, may be *mal-a-propos*, or in any way annoying. It is safest, when among strangers, to refrain from bitter animadversions on anybody.

INTRODUCING YOUR ACQUAINTANCES

In introducing a gentleman to a lady, address *her* first, as for instance—"Miss Smith, permit me to make you acquainted with Mr. Jones"—or, "Mrs. Farley, allow me to present Mr. Wilson"—that is, you must introduce the gentleman to the lady, rather than the lady to the gentleman. Also, if one lady is married and the other single, present the single lady to the matron, as—"Miss Thomson, let me introduce you to Mrs. Williams."

In introducing a foreigner, it is proper to present him as "Mr. Howard from England"—"Mr. Dupont from France"—"Mr. Wenzel from Germany." If you know of what European city he is a resident, it is better still, to say that he is "from London,"—"Paris,"—"Hamburg." Likewise, in introducing one of your own countrymen very recently returned from a distant part of the world, make him known as "Mr. Davis, just from China"—"Mr. Edwards, lately from Spain"—"Mr. Gordon, recently from South America." These slight specifications are easily made; and they afford, at once, an opening for conversation between the two strangers, as it will be perfectly natural to ask "the late arrived" something about the country he has last visited, or at least about his voyage.

PROPER PRONUNCIATION

An introduction should always be given in a distinct and audible voice, so that the name may be clearly understood. The purpose is defeated, if it is murmured over in so low a tone as to be unintelligible. And yet how often is this the case; for what reason it is difficult to divine. It is usual for the introducee to repeat the name of the introduced. This will prove that it has really been heard. For instance, if Mrs. Smith presents Miss Brook to Miss Miles, Miss Miles immediately says, "Miss Brook"—or better still— "Miss Brook, I am glad to meet you," or something similar. Miss Miles then begins a talk.

BE EXPLICIT

In introducing members of your own family, always mention, audibly, the name. It is not sufficient to say "my father," or "my mother"—"my son," "my daughter"— "my brother," or "my sister." There may be more than one surname in the same family. But say, "my father, Mr. Warton,"—"my daughter, Miss Wood"—or"my daughter-in-law, Mrs. Wood"—"my sister, Miss Mary

Ramsay"—"my brother, Mr. James Ramsay," &c. It is best in all these things to be explicit. The eldest daughter is usually introduced by her surname only—as "Miss Bradford"—her younger sisters, as "Miss Maria Bradford"—"Miss Harriet Bradford."

In presenting a clergyman, put the word "Reverend" before his name—unless he is a bishop, and then, of course, the word "Bishop" suffices. The head of a college-department introduce as "Professor"—and it is to them only that the title properly belongs, though arrogated by all sorts of public exhibitors, mesmerists and jugglers included.

FINDING THE PERFECT MATCH

Where the company is large, the ladies of the house should have tact enough to avoid introducing and placing together persons who cannot possibly assimilate, or take pleasure in each other's society. There can be no conversation that is mutually agreeable, between a real lady of true delicacy and refinement, and a so-called lady whose behaviour and talk are coarse and vulgar,— or between a woman of highly cultivated mind, and one who is grossly ignorant of every thing connected with books, and who boasts of that ignorance. We have heard a lady of fashion say, "Thank God, I never read." The answer might well have been, "You need not tell us that."

In inviting but a small company, it is indispensable to the pleasure of all, that you ask none who are strikingly unsuitable to the rest—or whose presence will throw a damp on conversation. Especially avoid bringing into the same room, persons who are at notorious enmity with each other, even if, unhappily, they should be members of the same family. Those who are known as adversaries should be invited on different evenings.

Avoid giving invitations to bores. They will come without.

REQUESTING AN INTRODUCTION

When you wish an introduction to a stranger lady, apply to your hostess, or to some of the family, or to one of the guests that is acquainted with that lady: you will then be led up and presented to her. Do not expect the stranger to be brought to you; it is your place to go to her.

If you are requested by a female friend to introduce her to a distinguished gentleman, a public character, be not so ungenerous as to go *immediately* and conspicuously to inform him of the fact. But spare her delicacy, by deferring the ceremony for a while; and then take an opportunity of saying to him, "I shall be glad to make you acquainted with my friend Miss Morris. Come with me, and I will introduce you." When the introduction has thus taken place, you may with propriety leave them together to entertain each other for awhile; particularly if both parties are capable of doing so. And then, after a quarter of an hour's conversation, let the lady release the gentleman from further attendance, by bowing to him, and turning to some other acquaintance who may not be far off. She can leave *him* much more easily than he can leave *her*, and it will be better to do so in proper time, than to detain him too long. It is generally in his power to return to her before the close of the evening, and if he is pleased with her society, he will probably make an opportunity of doing so.

If he is what is called a lion, consideration for the rest of the company should admonish her not to monopolise him. But lions usually know how to get away adroitly. By-the-bye, she must not talk to him of his professional celebrity, or ask him at once for his autograph.

We saw no less a person than Charles Dickens compelled, at a large party, to devote the whole evening to writing autographs for a multitude of young ladies— many of whom, not satisfied with obtaining one of his signatures for themselves, desired half a dozen others for "absent friends." All conversation ceased with the first requisition for an autograph. He had no chance of saying any thing. We were a little ashamed of our fair townswomen.

ADDRESSING YOUR SUPERIORS

Our countrymen abroad sometimes excite ill-concealed mirth, by the lavish use they make of titles when they chance to find themselves among the nobility. They should learn that none but servants or people of the lower classes make constant use of the terms "my lord," and "my lady"—"your lordship," or "your ladyship"— "your grace," &c., in conversing with persons of rank. Address them simply as Lord Derby, or Lord Dunmore— Lady Wilton, Lady Mornington, &c.

Chapter V

CONDUCT IN THE STREET

POSITION YOURSELF CORRECTLY

When three ladies are walking together, it is better for one to keep a little in advance of the other two, than for all three to persist in maintaining one unbroken line. They cannot all join in conversation without talking across each other—a thing that, in-doors or out-of-doors, is awkward, inconvenient, ungenteel, and should always be avoided. Also, three ladies walking abreast occupy too much of the pavement, and therefore incommode the other passengers. Three young *men* sometimes lounge along the pavement, arm in arm. Three young *gentlemen* never do so.

MEETING ACQUAINTANCES

If you meet a lady with whom you have become but slightly acquainted, and had merely a little conversation, (for instance, at a party or a morning visit,) and who moves in a circle somewhat higher or more fashionable than your own, it is safest to wait till she recognises you. Let her not see in you a disposition to obtrude yourself on her notice.

It is not expected that all intimacies formed at watering-places shall continue after the parties have returned to their homes. A mutual bow when meeting in the street is sufficient. But there is no interchanging of visits, unless both ladies have, before parting, testified a desire to continue the acquaintance. In this case, the lady who is eldest, or palpably highest in station, makes the first call. It is not customary for a young lady to make the first visit to a married lady.

When meeting them in the street, always speak first to your milliner, mantua-maker, seamstress, or to any one you have been in the practice of employing. To pass without notice any servant that you know, is rude and unfeeling, as they will attribute it to pride, not presuming to speak to you themselves, unless in reply. There are persons who having accepted, when in the country, much kindness from the country-people, are ashamed to recognise them when they come to town, on account of their rustic or unfashionable dress. This is a very vulgar, contemptible, and foolish pride; and is always seen through, and despised. There is no danger of plain country-people being mistaken for vulgar city-people. In our country, there is no reason for keeping aloof from any who are respectable in character and appearance. Those to be avoided are such as wear tawdry finery, paint their faces, and leer out of the corners of their eyes, *looking* disreputably, even if they are not disreputable in reality.

When a gentleman meets a lady with whom his acquaintance is very slight, (perhaps nothing more than a few words of talk at a party,) he allows her the option of continuing the acquaintance or not, at her pleasure; therefore, he waits till she recognises him, and till she evinces it by a bow,—he looking at her to give the opportunity. Thus, if she has no objection to numbering him among her acquaintances, she denotes it by bowing first. If she has any reason to disapprove of his character or habits, she is perfectly justifiable in "cutting" him, as it is termed. Let her bow very coldly the first time, and after that, not at all.

PAVEMENT ETIQUETTE

Young ladies should yield the wall to old ladies. Gentlemen do so to all ladies.

In some cities it is the custom for all gentlemen to give their arm to all ladies, when walking with them. In others, a gentleman's arm is neither offered nor taken, unless in the evening, on slippery pavements, or when the streets are very muddy. A lady only takes the arm of her husband, her affianced lover, or of her male relatives. In the country the custom is different. There, a gentleman, when walking with a lady, always gives her his arm; and is much offended when, on offering his arm, the lady refuses to take it. Still, if it is contrary to the custom of her place, she can explain it to him delicately, and he will at once see the propriety of her declining.

When a lady is walking between two gentlemen, she should divide her conversation as equally as practicable, or address most of it to him who is most of a stranger to her. He, with whom she is least on ceremony, will excuse her.

A gentleman on escorting a lady to her own home, must not leave her till he has rung the bell, and waited till the servant has come and opened the door, and till she is actually in the house. Men who know no better, think it sufficient to walk with her to the foot of the steps and there take their departure, leaving her to get in as she can.

If you stop a few minutes in the street to talk to an acquaintance, draw to one side of the pavement near the wall, so as not to impede the passengers—or you may turn and walk with her as far as the next corner. And never stop to talk in the middle of a crossing. To speak loudly in the street is exceedingly ungenteel, and foolish, as what you say will be heard by all who pass by. To call across the way to an acquaintance, is very unlady-like. It is best to hasten over, and speak to her, if you have any thing of importance to say.

TRAVELLING IN ADVERSE CONDITIONS

When a stranger offers to assist you across a brimming gutter, or over a puddle, or a glair of slippery ice, do not hesitate, or decline, as if you thought he was taking an unwarrantable liberty. He means nothing but civility. So accept it frankly, and thank him for it.

When you see persons slip down on the ice, do not laugh at them. There is no fun in being hurt, or in being mortified by a fall in the public street; and we know not how a *lady* can see any thing diverting in so painful a circumstance. It is more feminine, on witnessing such a sight, to utter an involuntary scream than a shout of laughter. And still more so, to stop and ascertain if the person that fell has been hurt.

TRAVELLING ON WHEELS

If, on stopping an omnibus, you find that a dozen people are already seated in it, draw back, and refuse to add to the number; giving no heed to the assertion of the driver, that "there is plenty of room." The *passengers* will not say so, and you have no right to crowd them all, even if you are willing to be crowded yourself—a thing that is extremely uncomfortable, and very injurious to your dress, which may, in consequence, be so squeezed and rumpled as never to look well again.

Have your sixpence ready in your fingers a few minutes before you are to get out; and you may request any gentleman near you to hand it up to the driver. So many accidents have happened from the driver setting off before a lady was entirely out  of the vehicle and safely landed in the street, that it is well to desire the gentleman not to hand up the sixpence till after you are fairly clear of the steps.

When expecting to ride in an omnibus, take care to have sufficient small change in your purse. We have seen, when a quarter-dollar has been handed up, and the driver was handing down the change, that it has fallen, and been scattered among the straw. There was no stopping to search for it, and therefore the ride cost twenty-five cents instead of six: the driver, of course, finding the change himself, as soon as he got rid of all his passengers.

It is most imprudent to ride in an omnibus with much money in your purse. Pickpockets of genteel appearance are too frequently among the passengers. We know a gentleman who in this way lost a pocket-book containing eighty dollars; and various ladies have had their purses taken from them, by well-dressed passengers. If you are obliged to have money of any consequence about you, keep your hand all the time in that pocket.

If the driver allows a drunken man to come into an omnibus, the ladies will find it best to get out; at least those whose seats are near his. It is, however, the duty of the gentlemen to insist on such fellows being refused admittance where there are ladies.

No lady should venture to ride in an omnibus after dark, unless she is escorted by a gentleman whom she knows. She had better walk home, even under the protection of a servant. If alone in an omnibus at night, she is liable to meet with improper company, and perhaps be insulted.

Chapter VI

SHOPPING

WHAT TO TAKE

When you go out shopping, it is well to take with you some *written* cards, inscribed with your residence as well as your name. For this purpose to use engraved visiting-cards is an unnecessary expense. That there may be no mistake, let your shopping-cards contain not only your street and number, but the side of the way, and between what streets your house is situated. Much inconvenience, disappointment, and delay have resulted from parcels being left at wrong places. If you are staying at a hotel, give also the number of your chamber, otherwise the package may be carried in mistake to the apartment of some other lady; the servants always knowing the number of the rooms, but not always remembering the names of the occupants; usually speaking of the ladies and gentlemen as No. 25, No. 42, &c.

There is another advantage in having cards with you when you go out shopping: if you should chance to forget your reticule, or handkerchief, and leave it on the counter, the shopkeeper will know exactly by the card where to send it, or for whom to keep it till called for.

ON PURCHASING AN ITEM

If you intend to purchase none but small articles, take but little money in your purse, so that if you chance to lose it, the loss may not be great.[3] When you buy articles of

---

[3] When circumstances render it expedient to carry much money out with you, divide it; putting half in one purse or pocket-book, and half in another, and put these portions into two pockets.

any consequence, they will always be sent home at your request—and (unless you keep a standing account at that store) desire the bill to be sent along; and sent at an hour when you will certainly be at hand to pay it. Be careful to take receipts for the payment; and keep the receipts on a file or wire. We have known instances when, from the clerk or storekeeper neglecting or delaying to cross out an account as soon as paid, the same bill was inadvertently sent twice over; and then by having the receipt to show, the necessity of *paying it twice over* was obviated. Look carefully at every item of the bill, and see that all is correct. Sometimes (though these oversights are of rare occurrence) the same article may accidentally be set down twice in the same bill. But this is easily rectified by taking the bill to the storekeeper, and showing it to him.

In subscribing for a magazine or newspaper, and paying in advance, (as you always should,) be especially careful of the receipts given to you at paying. So many persons are in the habit of allowing these accounts to run on for years, that if you neglect preserving your receipts, and cannot produce them afterward, you may be unintentionally classed among the delinquents, and have no means of proving satisfactorily that you have really paid.

A TIP FROM THE AUTHOR

Many ladies keep a day-book, in which they set down, regularly, all the money they have expended on that day; adding up the whole every week. An excellent plan, and of great importance to every one who is mistress of a family.

PURCHASING AN ITEM ON SOMEONE'S BEHALF

In making purchases for other persons, have bills made out; and send the bills (receipted) with the articles purchased, as an evidence of the exact price of the things, and that they were paid for punctually. The friends that have commissioned you to buy them, should *immediately* repay you. Much inconvenience may be felt by a lady whose command of money is small, when a friend living in a distant place, and probably in opulent circumstances, neglects or postpones the payment of these sums. She should, at the beginning, send money amply sufficient to make these purchases. It is enough that you take the trouble of going to the stores, selecting the desired articles, and having them packed and sent off. She has no right to put you to the slightest pecuniary inconvenience. There have been instances, where articles thus bought for a lady in a far-off place, have not been paid for by that lady till after the lapse of many months. For such remissness there is no excuse. To go shopping for a friend is rarely a pleasant business. Besides its encroaching on your time, there is always a danger of the purchases proving unsatisfactory, or not suiting the taste of her for whom they are intended. Also, circumstances may prevent the articles reaching her as soon as expected. Whenever practicable, it is best to send all such packages by the Transportation Line—that charge to be paid by the owner, on delivery.

It is not well to trouble a gentleman with the care of a parcel, unless it is quite small, and he has to pass the door of the house at which it is to be delivered; or unless his residence is in the immediate neighbourhood.

BROWSING ETIQUETTE

When visiting the shops, if you do not intend to buy at that time, but are merely looking round to see varieties of articles before you determine on what to purchase, candidly say so to the persons standing at the counter. They will (particularly if they know you) be perfectly willing to show you such things as you desire to see, in the hope that you may return to their store and buy of them afterward. At the same time, avoid giving unnecessary trouble; and do not, from mere curiosity, desire such things to be brought to you as you have no intention of buying at all.

WARDROBE WISDOM

The practice that is called cheapening, or beating down the price, is now nearly obsolete. Most tradesmen have a fixed price for every thing, and will not abate.

It is but rarely that you will meet with articles of really good quality on very low terms, unless near the close of the season, when the storekeepers, anxious to get rid of their old stock, generally put down the prices of the goods that are left on hand; knowing that by the return of next season, these will be superseded by things of a newer fashion. Economical ladies, who are not resolutely determined on wearing none but articles of the very latest fashion, may thus supply themselves with excellent silks, lawns, &c. in August and September, at prices far below what they would have given in May or June. And then they can lay them by till next summer. In the same way they can purchase merinoes, mousselines de laine, &c. in January, February, and March, much lower than in November and December. It is best always to buy rather too much than too little; and to have a piece left, rather than to get a scanty pattern, such as will barely hold out, leaving nothing for repairs or alterations. There is much advantage in getting an extra yard and a half, or two yards, and keeping it back for new sleeves. Unless you are small and slender, it is not well to buy a dress embroidered with a border pattern. They are always scanty in width, and have that look when made up. The skirts are never quite wide enough. A tall woman requires as full a skirt as a fat one; else her height will make her look lanky and narrow.

MADE TO FIT

When bespeaking an article to be made purposely for you, ascertain from the maker what will be the cost, and then request him to write down the terms on a card, or a slip of paper, or on a leaf of your tablet. If he says he cannot tell how much it will be, or that he knows not what price to fix on it, or that he cannot decide till after it is finished, it will be safest and wisest for you to decline engaging it, till he *has* calculated the amount, or something very near it. Persist in this condition being a *sine qua non*. It is his place to know every thing connected with his business, and to be able to judge of his outlay, and his profits.

If you do not insist on a satisfactory answer when making the bargain, you may in the end find yourself greatly overcharged, (as we know by experience;) the price in the bill, after the article is made, and sent home, proving infinitely higher than you would have been willing to give if previously aware of it. In dealing with foreigners whose language is not yours, take especial care that there is a correct understanding on both sides.

SHOPPING AWAY FROM HOME

When on a visit to a city with which you are not familiar, enquire where the best shops are to be found, and make memorandums of them in your tablets. This will spare your friends the trouble of accompanying you on your shopping expeditions. And if you have a small pocket-map of the town, there will be no danger of losing your way. Except to ladies whose chief delight is in seeing things connected with dress, to go shopping with a stranger is usually very tiresome. Also, the stranger will feel less constraint by going alone; and more at liberty to be guided by her own taste in selecting, and to consult her pecuniary convenience in regard to the price. It is only when you feel that you have reason for distrusting your own judgment, as to the quality and gentility of the articles, that it is well to be accompanied by a person of more experience. And then you will, most probably, be unwilling to fatigue her by going to as many shops as you would like to visit. In most cases, it is best to go shopping without any companion, except, perhaps, a member of your immediate family. Gentlemen consider it a very irksome task to go on shopping expeditions, and their ill-concealed impatience becomes equally irksome to you.

A TIP FROM THE AUTHOR

If you have given the salesman or saleswoman unusual trouble in showing you articles which you find not to suit, make some compensation, by at least one or two small purchases before leaving the store; for instance, linen to lay by as a body-lining for a future dress, gloves, mits, a neck-ribbon, cotton spools, pins, needles, tape, black sewing-silk, &c.,— things that will always come into use.

EXAMPLES OF AN UNTOWARD CUSTOMER

There are still some ladies who think that one of the great arts of shopping, is to disparage the articles shown to them, to exclaim at the price, and to assert that at other places they can get exactly such things infinitely lower. When shopping, (as well as under all other circumstances,) it is best to adhere to the truth. If you really like the article, why not gratify the salesman by saying so. If you know that the price is in conformity to the usual rate, you need not attempt to get it lower, for you will seldom succeed—unless, indeed, on that day the tradesman is particularly anxious to sell, having a sum of money to make up, and being somewhat at a loss. Perhaps then, he may abate something; but if he does not himself propose the abatement, and if he is largely in business, and sure of plenty of custom, there will be little use in your urging it.

If you are a stranger in the city, (Philadelphia for instance,) do not always be exclaiming at the prices, and declaring that you can buy the same articles much lower and much handsomer in New York, Boston, or Baltimore. For certain reasons, prices are different in different places. If an article is shown to you in Philadelphia as "something quite new," refrain from saying that it has been out of fashion these two years in New York. This may injure its sale with bystanders, chancing to hear you. You need only say "that it is very pretty, but you do not want it now."

When you see on another lady a new article of dress that you admire, it is *not* ill-manners, (but rather the contrary,) to tell her so. But unless you really desire to get one exactly like it for yourself, and are sincerely asking for information, it is considered very rude to enquire where she bought it, and what was the cost. And it is peculiarly vulgar to preface the enquiry by the foolish words—"If it is a fair question." The very doubt proves that you know the question to be a very unfair one. And so it is. We have never known that expression used except to introduce something rude and improper. Any lady who is asked an impertinent question, would be perfectly justifiable in saying, "Excuse me from answering"—and then immediately changing the conversation. Yet there are ladies who are always catechising others about their dress. You are not bound to give explicit answers to these, or any other questions concerning your personal affairs.

Much mischief accrues in society, from some ladies being too inquisitive, and others too communicative.

BARGAIN HUNTING

It is really a great fatigue, both of body and mind, to go shopping with a very close economist, particularly if you know that she can well afford a sufficiently liberal expenditure. The length of time she will ponder over every thing before she can "make up her mind;" the ever-besetting fear that she may possibly have to give a few cents more in one store than in another; her long deliberation as to whether a smaller than the usual quantity may not be "made to do;" her predilection for bargain-seeking in streets far off, and ungenteel; the immense trouble she gives to the persons behind the counter,—all will induce you to forswear trying a second time the experiment of attending on the progress of a shopper who sets out with the vain expectation of obtaining good articles at paltry prices.

In what are called "cheap shops," you will rarely find more than two or three things that are really cheap. If of bad quality, they are not *cheap*, but dear. Low-priced ribbons, for instance, are generally flimsy, tawdry, of ugly figures, and vulgar colours,—soon fading, and soon "getting into a string." Yet there are ladies who will walk two miles to hustle in the crowd they find squeezing toward the counter of the last new emporium of cheap ribbons; and, while waiting their turn, have nothing to look at around them but lots of trash, that if they bought they would be ashamed to wear. Coarse finery is trumpery.

On the other hand, for ladies of small means, it is not indispensable to their standing in society, that they should deal only at stores noted for selling *higher* than the usual price. It is a very poor boast; particularly when they cannot afford it.

ALL IS IN THE DETAIL

Whatever may be the caprices of fashion, a lady of good taste (and we may add, good sense,) will not, in buying dresses, select those of large figures, and high glaring colours. There is something peculiarly ungenteel and ungraceful in a white ground with large red flowers and green leaves wandering over it. Even if the fabric is brocade, it has a look of calico. Red and green is only beautiful in real flowers. In a lady's dress, it somehow looks unlady-like. A great variety of bright colours is only suited to a carpet. For a dress, two are quite sufficient. And then if one is blue, pink, scarlet, or orange, let it be contrasted with brown, gray, olive, or some chaste and quiet tint that will set it off. Few silks are more becoming than those in which the figure is formed by a darker shade of the same colour as the ground. Silks of one colour only, trim the best—variegated trimming looks confused and ineffective. No colours are more ungenteel, or in worse taste, than reddish lilacs, reddish purples, and reddish browns. The original tint of aronetta, or anatto, is the contempt of ladies; but by previously washing the article in strong, warm pot-ash water, before it is put into the solution of aronetta, you will obtain a beautiful bird-of-paradise colour, entirely free from all appearance of the unpopular powder.

Buy no silk that is stiff and hard, however thick and heavy it may seem. It will crack and split, and wear worse than a soft silk that appears much thinner. Venture on no satin that is not of excellent quality. A thin satin frays and ravels, and is not worth making up. Never use satin to cover cord. It ravels too much. Velvet and satin should be corded with substantial silk. If you cannot match the exact shade, let it be darker rather than lighter. A belt-ribbon should always be darker than the dress. Cord merino with itself. A cording of silk will not wash.

If you cannot get lace that is tolerably fine, wear none at all, rather than have it coarse. We have seen lace called Brussels, so coarse that it looked as if made of cotton, though in truth it was of thread. There was no real beauty in it. Genuine Brussels lace is exquisitely fine.

Large showy ornaments, by way of jewellery, are exceedingly ungenteel. They always tell their own story, of glass stones set in gilding, not gold. If you cannot obtain real jewels, never attempt sham ones. It requires no practised eye to detect them—particularly false diamonds.

PEACEFUL SHOPPING

Do not interfere with the shopping of other customers, (who may chance to stand near you at the counter,) by either praising or deprecating any of the articles they are looking at. Leave them to the exercise of their own judgment; unless they ask your opinion. And then give it in a low voice, and sincerely.

If you meet an acquaintance unexpectedly in a store, it is not well to engage in a long conversation with her, and thus detain persons behind the counter from waiting on other customers. Finish your purchase-making first, and then you will have leisure to step aside and converse. A store is not the place for social intercourse, and you may chance to say something there, that bystanders should not hear. "Greetings in the market-place" should always be short.

CUSTOMER SATISFACTION

And now a few words to saleswomen. They have always, when commencing that vocation, two important qualities to cultivate (exclusive of cleverness in business)—civility, and patience. Let them also learn activity in moving, and quickness in recollecting where all the articles called for are to be found, so as not to keep the customers waiting too long, while they, the sellers, are searching the shelves and boxes. Also, if a lady wishes to match something, (for instance, a piece of silk,) it is foolish and useless to bring her a piece that is not *exactly* like; trying to persuade her to take it, and calling it "as good a match as she is likely to get." Of course she will *not* take a piece that is only *tolerably* like, but not quite the same; for unless it matches exactly, it is no match at all. If a customer enquires for light blue ribbon it is absurd to bring her dark blue, saying "we have no light blue"—or to say "we have no pink, but we have scarlet— we have no lilac, but we have purple." Or still worse, to try to persuade the customer that deep crimson is a beautiful shade of scarlet; or worse than all, that those very unbecoming tints, called improperly rose-white and pearl-white, are really a pure dead white; when you know very well that they are no such thing. Both white and black are very difficult to match *precisely*.

Every female who keeps, or attends in a store, should discourage the visits of her friends at business hours. If she looks off to chat with her shop-visiters, she cannot attend properly to her customers; and those visiters may be inconsiderate and obtrusive enough to interfere, by putting in their word, and praising the beauty or cheapness of the articles, by way of promoting the interest of the seller, which it ultimately *will not*.

Show as much civility and attention to a customer plainly dressed, and walking on foot, or getting out of an omnibus, as you would to a lady elegantly attired, and coming in her own carriage. The former may prove the most profitable customer. Be careful to exhibit no temper, even if you have had the trouble of showing a variety of goods to one who goes away without buying any thing. Another time, perhaps, she may come and make large purchases: but if you offend her, she will assuredly never enter the store again. Recollect that no one feels under the least compulsion to buy what does not suit them. You would not yourself. Habitual courtesy is a valuable qualification, and always turns to good account.

Chapter VII

TRAVELLING

TRAVELLING ESSENTIALS

No lady should set out on a journey unprovided with an oiled-silk bag for the reception of tooth-brushes, soap, a hair-brush, and a towel. Let the bag be about half a quarter of a yard longer at the back than at the front; so as to leave a flap to turn over, and tie down, when all the articles are in. It should be square, (exclusive of the flap,) and about a quarter and half-quarter in length, and the same in breadth; stitched in compartments, something like an old-fashioned thread-case, only that the compartments differ much in size. The two smallest are for two tooth-brushes. Another should be broad enough to contain a hair-brush. For travelling, have a hair-brush with a mirror at the back, and if you can get one that has also a dressing-comb attached to it, so much the better. The largest compartment (which should occupy the centre) is for a towel, and a cake of soap. If you are obliged to start in haste, all these things can be put in while wet from recent use, the towel being rolled or folded into as small a compass as possible. The oiled silk will prevent the wet from oozing through. When all are in, turn over the flap at the top, (which should be furnished with two long strings of broad, white tape,) and tie it securely down. Carry this bag in the square satchel which all ladies now keep in their hands when travelling, and which contain such things as they may want during the day, precluding the necessity of opening their large carpet-bag, till they stop for the night.

In a carpet-bag pack nothing but white articles, or such as can be washed, and will not be spoiled by the bag chancing to get wet. Have your name engraved on the lock of your carpet-bag, and also on the brass plate of your trunks. Besides this, write your full direction on several cards, make a small hole in each, and running a string through the hole, tie a card to the handle of each trunk, and sew one on the side of your carpet-bag—the direction designating the place to which you are going. Your name in full should be painted in white letters on every trunk. This costs but a trifle, and secures the recognition of your baggage when missing. It is also an excellent plan to tie round the handle of each trunk or bag, a bit of ribbon—blue, red, or yellow—all the bits being off the same piece.[4]

Write on a large card, a list and description of each trunk, box, &c. and give the card to the gentleman who escorts you. It will greatly assist him in identifying all the articles that comprise your baggage.

BEFORE YOU SET OFF

Be quite ready at least a quarter of an hour before the time for starting. Nelson said he traced all the most fortunate events of his life to his practice of being, on every occasion, quite prepared a quarter of an hour too early. It is a good rule.

Previous to departing, put into the hand of your escort rather more than a sufficient sum for the expenses of your journey, so as to provide for all possible contingencies. He

---

[4] In a former work of the author's, *The House Book*, published by A. Hart, Philadelphia, will be found ample directions for packing trunks, &c.

will return you the balance when all is paid. Having done this, should any person belonging to the line come to you for your fare, refer them to the gentleman, (mentioning his name,) and take care to pay nothing more yourself.

TRAVELLING ATTIRE

Dress very plainly when travelling. Few ladies that *are* ladies wear finery in rail-cars, and steamboats—still less in stages—stage-roads being usually very dusty. Showy silks, and what are called dress-bonnets are preposterous— so are jewellery ornaments, which, if real, you run a great risk of losing, and if false, are very ungenteel. Above all, do not travel in white kid gloves. Respectable women never do.

The best travelling-dresses are of merino, or alpaca; plain mousseline de laine, grey or brown linen; or strong India silk, senshaw for instance. In warm weather, gingham is better than printed lawn, which rumples and tumbles and "gets into a string" directly. The sleeves wide, for if tight to the arm, they will stain with perspiration. Your travelling-dress for summer should have a large cape or pelerine of the same. Beside which, carry on your arm a large shawl for chilly mornings and evenings. No lady should travel in cold weather, without a warm cloak, mantilla, or pelisse,—furs, &c. of course— and travelling-boots lined with fur or flannel; having also inner soles of lambs-wool, varnished on the leather side to make them water-proof. Take with you one of those very useful umbrellas, that are large enough to shelter one person from the rain, and can also be used as a parasol. Do not pack it away in a trunk, for you may want it in the transit from rail-car to steamboat. Keep it near you all the time, with your satchel and extra shawl. By all means wear a white collar.

TRAVELLING BY RAIL-CAR

If you are fortunately able to ride backward as well as forward, you will be less incommoded with flying sparks, by sitting with your back to the engine. A spark getting into the eye is very painful, and sometimes dangerous. It is possible to expel it by blowing your nose very hard, while with the other hand you wipe out the particle of cinder with a corner of your handkerchief, pulling down the lower eye-lid. We have seen this done successfully. Another way is to wrap the head of a pin in the corner of a fine, soft cambric handkerchief, and placing it beneath the lid, sweep all round the eye with it. If this does not succeed, get out at the first station-house where you can stop long enough, procure a bristle-hair from a sweeping-brush, tie it in a loop or bow with a bit of thread, and let some one insert it beneath your eye-lid, and move it slowly all round, so as to catch in it the offending particle of coal, and bring it out. Or if there is time, send to the nearest apothecary for an eye-stone, (in reality, a lobster's eye,) and soak it five minutes in a saucer of vinegar and water to give it activity, then, wiping it dry, and carefully inserting it beneath the eye-lid, bind a handkerchief over it. The eye-stone will go circling round the eye, and most likely take up the mote in its course. When the pain ceases, remove the handkerchief, and wash the eye with cold water.

To read in a rail-car is very injurious to the eyes, from the quivering, tremulous motion it seems to communicate to the letters of the page. It is best to abstain from your book till you are transferred to the steamboat.

Many persons cannot talk in a rail-car without a painful exertion of the voice. And it is not an easy task, even to those whose lungs are strong. You can easily excuse yourself from conversing with your escort, by telling him that your voice is not loud enough to be heard above the racket of the cars, and that though you will gladly listen to *him*, he must allow you to listen without replying, except in as few words as possible. If he finds a gentleman with whom he is acquainted, desire him to talk to his friend, and leave you to hear their conversation as a silent auditor.

A TIP FROM THE AUTHOR

In arriving at a rail-road depôt, be careful not to quit the cars till after they have positively stopped quite still. The time gained is but an instant, and the risk is very imminent of serious injury by falling, should your ankle twist in stepping out while there is the least motion.

TRAVELLING BY STEAMBOAT

If you pass the night in a steamboat, and can afford the additional expense of a *whole* state-room, by all means engage one as soon as you go on board. The chambermaid will give you the key and the number, and you can retire to it whenever you please, and enjoy the luxury of being alone, and of washing and dressing without witnesses. If you are constrained to take a berth in the ladies' sleeping-cabin, it is not the least necessary to retire to it immediately after supper. By doing so you will have a very long, tiresome night, and be awake many hours before morning. And if you are awake, do not be continually calling upon the poor chambermaid, and disturbing her with enquiries, such as "Where are we now?" and "How soon shall we arrive?"

The saloon is the place in which ladies and gentlemen sit together. If a lady is so inconsiderate or selfish as to violate the rules of the boat, by inviting her husband or lover to take a seat in the ladies' cabin, there is no impropriety in sending the chambermaid to remind him that he must leave the room. This is often done, and always should be. We once saw a gentleman (or a pretended one) so pertinacious in remaining, (it is true his lady-love urged him "not to mind,") that the captain had to be brought to threaten him with forcible expulsion. This had the desired effect.

Such are the facilities of travelling, that a lady evidently respectable, plainly dressed, and behaving properly, may travel very well without a gentleman. Two ladies still better. On commencing the journey she should speak to the conductor, requesting him to attend to her and her baggage, and to introduce her to the captain of the boat, who will of course take charge of her during the voyage.

Before arriving at the wharf, she had best engage one of the servants of the boat, (promising him a shilling or two,) to obtain for her a porter or a hack, and to see that her baggage is safe. She must stipulate with the hackman that no stranger is to be put into the carriage with her. This is against the law, but notwithstanding, is often done, and the lady who has first engaged the coach, is liable to have for her riding-companions persons of improper character and vulgar appearance, and to be carried with them to their places in remote parts of the city, before she is conveyed to her own home. Previous to getting in, take the number of the coach, by writing it on a card with your pencil, and make your bargain with him as to the charge for conveying you and your baggage.

It would be well if the imposition and insolence of hack-drivers were *always* followed with the punishments provided by law. Ladies are naturally unwilling to appear at a magistrate's office. But it is the duty of every gentleman, as a good citizen, to see that the municipal regulations are never violated with impunity.

All trouble may be avoided on arriving, by sending for the captain of the boat, and requesting him to see you on shore, or to depute his clerk to that office.

Chapter VIII

DEPORTMENT AT A HOTEL, OR AT A LARGE BOARDING-HOUSE

JUDGING EYES

Now that there is so much travelling in the summer, (and indeed at all seasons,) and so much living in public, to save the trouble and the expense of keeping house in private, it may be well to offer some hints on the propriety of manners that ought to be observed in places where you are always exposed to the inspection and to the remarks of strangers. These strangers, knowing you but slightly, or not at all, will naturally draw their inferences for or against you from what they see before their eyes; concluding that you are genteel or ungenteel, patrician or plebeian, according to the coarseness or the polish of your manners.

Yet strange to say, there are persons who indulge themselves in astounding acts of rudeness, from the supposition that a hotel is only a tavern, a sort of Liberty Hall, where every one has a right to "take their ease in their inn," if they pay for it. Have they no respect for themselves?

BREAKFASTING

It is usual for members of the same party to meet in the ladies' drawing-room before they go in to breakfast, unless the party is large; and then it is not expected that half a dozen persons should be kept waiting for one or two late risers, or tardy dressers. When two or three of the party find themselves ready in the parlour, it will be best for them to proceed to the eating-room, and leave the others to follow at their convenience, by twos or by threes,—always seeing that a young lady, if a stranger, is not left to go in alone.

Strangers at hotels can have no particular seats at breakfast and tea, as at these two repasts, they always come to table by instalments, and at no regular time. If a large party enters all at once and they are *determined* to sit all together, they may occasion much inconvenience to persons already seated, or to the regular boarders, who have their allotted seats. Neither is there any necessity or advantage in six, eight, or ten people, who travel as one party, resolving to establish themselves at a hotel-table all side by side, in a row; particularly when it causes inconvenience to others. Certainly not more than three or four persons ranged in a line can join in the same conversation, or attend to the wants of their friends.

Nine o'clock (or half-past) is the latest hour that any guest at a hotel should come to breakfast; and few *Americans* have so little consideration as to detain the table and the servants till ten or eleven.[5] At a boarding-house, the guests are very soon made to understand that if they are late risers, they need expect nothing but the cold leavings of the breakfast. At a hotel they find more indulgence.

Speak to the waiter in a distinct, but not in too loud a voice, and always civilly. Thank him for any little extra attention he may show you. If you do not like what he has brought you, or find that you cannot eat it, make your objection in a low voice, so as not to be heard by the

---

[5] Nevertheless, it is not good manners to make any remark (even to a friend) on their coming to breakfast late or early. It is no concern of yours, and they have reasons of their own, undoubtedly.

neighbouring guests; and quietly desire him to bring you something else.

It is usual at a hotel-table for each waiter to have charge of three or four persons, and to attend to *their* wants exclusively. If you are a stranger, ask the waiter his name when he first comes to you; and unless he is not at hand, and you see another standing idle, do not call on any one else to attend you.

It is ungenteel to go to the breakfast-table in any costume approaching to full dress. There must be no flowers or ribbons in the hair. A morning-cap should be as simple as possible. The most genteel morning-dress is a close gown of some plain material, with long sleeves, which in summer may be white muslin.

A TIP FROM THE AUTHOR

The fashion of wearing black silk mittens at breakfast is now obsolete. It was always inconvenient, and neither useful nor ornamental.

SECURITY

After breakfast, it is customary for the ladies to adjourn to the drawing-room, where they converse, or read the papers, or receive early visiters, while the chambermaids are putting the bed-chambers in order. Some who are not accustomed to hotels, go immediately from the breakfast-table to their own apartment, sitting there among the flue and dust during the whole process of bed-making and room-sweeping; afraid to trust the chambermaid alone, lest she should steal something. This is absurd. They should know that the chambermaids (being all considered honest and responsible) are furnished with duplicate keys, by which they can at any time unlock the chamber-doors, and let themselves in, when the occupant is absent. Also, this palpable suspicion of their honesty is an insult to the girls, and is always felt as such. It is sufficient to lock the bureau, the wardrobe, and your trunks. When you go out, (that is, out of the house,) *then* lock the door of your room, lest some one passing by, should have curiosity to stroll in and look about, and meddle with what they see there.

HELPING A FELLOW LADY

Should you perceive that the dress of another lady is, by some accident, out of order—for instance, that a hook or a button has become unfastened; or that a string is visibly hanging out; a collar unpinned, and falling off; the corner of a shawl dragging along the floor; a skirt caught up; or a sleeve slipping down, immediately have the kindness to apprise her of it in a low voice, and assist her in repairing the mischance; and, if necessary, leave the room with her for that purpose.

We have seen a lady who, finding that a cluster of her false curls was coming down, had the courage to say so to a gentleman with whom she was conversing at a party. And going openly, and at once, to the nearest mirror, she calmly adjusted her borrowed locks, and returned to her seat with a good grace. Consequently, nobody laughed at the untoward accident; as might perhaps have been the case, had she seemed excessively confused and mortified, and awkwardly tried to hold on her curls till she got out of the room.

CHOOSING YOUR CONVERSATIONS CAREFULLY

There is no impropriety in a lady commencing conversation with a stranger of genteel appearance. You can easily take occasion to mention your own name, and then, in return, she will communicate hers. But, unless you are previously certain of her respectability, have little to say to a woman who is travelling without a companion, and whose face is painted, who wears a profusion of long curls about her neck, who has a meretricious expression of eye, and who is over-dressed. It is safest to avoid her. Also, you will derive no pleasure or advantage from making acquaintance with females who are evidently coarse and vulgar, even if you know that they are rich, live in a large house, and are of respectable character. Young girls who are loud, noisy, bold, and forward, (however fashionable they may be,) it is best also to avoid. They will not want your society, as they are generally all the time surrounded by "beaux," or else rattling over the keys of the piano.

RING FOR ASSISTANCE

If you want pen and ink, or any sort of stationery, you can obtain it immediately, by ringing for a servant to bring it you from the office. In ringing the bell, one pull is sufficient; and always pull the cord *downward*. If you jerk it out horizontally, and give successively several hard pulls in that direction, the cord is very likely to break, or the knob or tassel to come off in your hand. At the chief hotel in one of the New England cities, we saw a printed paper with directions in large type, pasted beside *every bell-pull in the house*; the directions specifying minutely the proper mode of bell-ringing. Could it be that this house was frequented by persons unaccustomed to bells?

MAKING A RACKET

To return to the too-prevalent evil of uninvited and ill-timed piano-playing, (much of which does not deserve the name of music,) we have always been at a loss to understand how a young stranger, (modest and unobtrusive in other things,) could walk up to the instrument, sometimes almost as soon as she arrives, and rattle "fast and furious" over the keys, drowning the voices of ladies and gentlemen who were talking, and therefore compelling them to cease their conversation; or if they pursued it, obliging them to raise their tone painfully; or to lose more than half, from the impossibility of hearing each other distinctly.

To read when piano-playing is going on, is to most persons impossible. There are few readers who cannot so concentrate their attention on their book, as not to be disturbed by any *talking* that may occur in their vicinity; and if talking *does* withdraw their attention from the book, it is best that they should read only when alone in their apartment. But we have met with no one who could read in the neighbourhood of a played piano.

If the music is really very good, and accompanied by a fine voice, it is true that most readers will willingly close the book to listen. But if the playing is barely tolerable, or decidedly bad, and if the singing is weak and insipid, or harsh and screaming, or timeless and tasteless, who can possibly wish to hear it; except perhaps a doating father, or an injudicious mother, vain of her daughter because she is *hers*, and so anxious to show her off, that she encourages the girl to display even her deficiencies.

We repeat that no lady should play or sing in company, unless she knows herself to be universally considered a good singer or player, and capable of something more than the mere series of lessons she has learnt from her music teacher. Also, some punishment should be devised for a young girl who cannot play, yet has the folly and assurance to seat herself at the piano of a public parlour, and annoy the company by an hour of tinking and tanking with one finger only. Yet this we have seen; and her mother present all the time.

ACTING THE FOOL

In conversing with gentlemen at hotels, (and all other places,) try not to fall into the too common practice of talking to him nothing but nonsense. It is a problem difficult to solve, that so many ladies of good abilities and cultivated minds, and who always with their own sex talk like intelligent, sensible women, should, as soon as they get into conversation with a gentleman, seem immediately to take leave of rationality, and demean themselves like utter fools—giving way at once to something they call *excitement*, now the fashionable word for almost every feeling that is wrong.

We grieve to see a charming, modest, refined young lady, almost the moment a gentleman begins to talk to her, changing her whole demeanour, and quickly becoming bold, forward, noisy, and nonsensical; chattering at the top of her voice about nothing; and keeping up a continual laugh about nothing. Does she suppose he cannot understand her if she talks sense,— or does she think he will like her the better for regaling him with nothing but folly? On the contrary, we are glad to see vivacity in women of all ages; and if they have a sprinkling of wit and humour, so much the better. But those who have not a talent for wit and humour, had best not attempt it. Again, in listening to a woman of real wit, you will see that it is her hearers who laugh, and not herself.

Persons who have no turn for humour, and little perception of it, are apt to mistake mere coarseness for that amusing gift; and in trying to be diverting, often become vulgar—a word not too severe for things that are sometimes said and written by very good people who wish to be funny, and do not know how. For instance, there is no wit, but there is shocking ungentility, in a lady to speak of taking a "snooze" instead of a nap,—in calling pantaloons "pants," or gentlemen "gents,"—in saying of a man whose dress is getting old that he looks "seedy,"—and in alluding to an amusing anecdote, or a diverting incident, to say that it is "rich." All slang words are detestable from the lips of ladies.

NO SMALL DOGS ALLOWED

If you own a lap-dog or poodle, recollect that however charming it may be to yourself, others may regard it as an annoyance; therefore, try to do without it when you are in the parlour of a house that is not your own, and when the company present does not consist entirely of your own family. All but their infatuated mistresses soon become very tired of the society of these animals. Poodles are generally peevish, whining, and snappish, prone to get under chairs and bite at feet, and to writhe about the skirts of dresses.

Chapter IX

HOTEL DINNER

BEING SEATED

If you and your party are strangers, recently arrived, do not at once take the lead, and walk up to the head of the table, regardless of dislodging and causing inconvenience among the regular boarders, to whom those seats have been allotted. But desire a servant to show you a place. The head-waiter is usually at hand to arrange seats for the strangers, and he will attend to you. Persons not accustomed to hotels, frequently show a great craving for the seats near the head of the table. This is foolish. There are no places of honour; neither are the eatables better at one part of the table than another.

WAIT FOR YOUR WAITER

Do not attempt removing a cover from a dish, that you may help yourself before the rest of the company. Leave all that to the waiters. Tell them what you want in a distinct, but not in a loud, conspicuous voice. In asking a servant to bring you a thing, add not the useless and senseless words "*will* you?" for instance, "Bring me the bread, will you?"— "Give me some water, will you?" Of course he will. Has he the option of refusing? How you would be startled were he to answer, "*I will not.*"

If in turning to speak to a waiter, you find him in the act of serving some one else, say, "*When you are at leisure, I will thank you for some water,*"—or whatever you may want.

It is selfish to be continually sending out of the room the man who waits near you, for the purpose of bringing extra things for yourself. Try to be satisfied with what you find on the table, and recollect that you are depriving others of his services, while you are dispatching him back and forward on errands to the kitchen.

USING CUTLERY

Many persons hold silver forks awkwardly, as if not accustomed to them. It is fashionable to use your knife only while cutting up the food small enough to be eaten with the fork alone. While cutting, keep the fork in your left hand, the hollow or concave side downward, the fork in a very slanting position, and your fore-finger extended far down upon its handle. When you have done cutting up what you are going to eat, lay aside your knife, transfer the fork to your right hand, and take a small piece of bread in your left. If eating any thing soft, use your silver fork somewhat as a spoon, turning up the hollow side that the cavity may hold the food. If engaged in talking, do not, meanwhile, hold your fork bolt upright, but incline it downward, so as to be nearly on a level with your plate. Remember, always, to keep your own knife, fork, and spoon out of the dishes. It is an insult to the company, and a disgrace to yourself, to dip into a dish any thing that has been even for a moment in your mouth. To take butter or salt with your own knife is an abomination. There is always a butter-knife and a salt-spoon. It is nearly as bad to take a lump of sugar with your fingers.

A MOUTHFUL OF MANNERS

No lady looks worse than when gnawing a bone, even of game or poultry. Few *ladies* do it. In fact, nothing should be sucked or gnawed in public; neither corn bitten off from the cob, nor melon nibbled from the rind.[6] It is very ungraceful to eat an orange at table, unless, having cut a bit off the top, you eat the inside with a tea-spoon—otherwise reserve it for the privacy of your own room. Always pare apples and peaches; and crack no nuts with your teeth. In eating cherries, put your half-closed hand before your mouth to receive the stones; then lay them on one side of your plate. To spit out the stones one at a time as you proceed with the cherries is very ungenteel. Get rid of plumb-stones in the same manner.

CHOOSING A DISH

If you are helped to any thing whose appearance you do not like, or in which you are disappointed when you taste it, you, of course, at a hotel table, are not obliged to eat it. Merely leave it on your plate, without audibly giving the reason; and then, in a low voice, desire the waiter to bring you something else. It is well, while at table, to avoid any discussion of the demerits of the dishes. On the other hand, you may praise them as much as you please.

---

[6] It is, however, customary in eating sweet potatoes of a large size, to break them in two, and taking a piece in your hand, to pierce down to the bottom with your fork, and then mix in some butter, continuing to hold it thus while eating it.

In refusing to be helped to any particular thing, never give as a reason that "you are afraid of it," or "that it will disagree with you." It is sufficient simply to *refuse*; and then no one has a right to ask why?

INAPPROPRIATE DISCOURSE

While at table, all allusions to dyspepsia, indigestion, or any other disorders of the stomach, are vulgar and disgusting. The word "stomach" should never be uttered at any table, or indeed anywhere else, except to your physician, or in a private conversation with a female friend interested in your health. It is a disagreeable word, (and so are all its associations,) and should never be mentioned in public to "ears polite." Never, while at table, (whether in public or private,) allow yourself to talk on painful or disgusting subjects. Avoid all discussions of sicknesses, sores, surgical operations, dreadful accidents, shocking cruelties, or horrible punishments. A love of such topics, evinces a coarse and unfeminine mind. It is rude in gentlemen at any time to introduce them before ladies; and a polished man never does so. The conversation at table should be as cheerful and pleasant as possible. Political and sectarian controversies ought to have no place there. Shakespeare truly says, "Unquiet meals make ill digestion."

Avoid the discussion at table of private affairs; either your own, or those of other people. Remember that "servants have ears," and frequently much more quickness of comprehension and retentiveness of memory than is generally supposed. So have children.

EXAMPLES OF BAD MANNERS

Abstain from picking your teeth at table. Notwithstanding that custom has allowed this practice in Europe, (even in fashionable society,) it is still a very disagreeable one, and to delicate spectators absolutely sickening to behold. Delay it till you are alone, and till you can indulge in it without witnesses. We know that it is quite possible to go on through a long life, and to have clean teeth, without ever once having been *seen* to pick them; and yet those teeth are really picked after every meal.

Should you chance to be extremely incommoded by some extraneous substance that has gotten between your teeth, you can remove it unperceived, by holding up your napkin or handkerchief before your mouth, so as effectually to conceal the process. When you take any thing out of your teeth, do not make the persons who are near you sick, by laying the disgusting particle on the side of your plate; but conceal it immediately. Still, nothing but "sheer necessity" can excuse any teeth-picking at table.

We have seen a young *lady*, at a very fashionable house in one of our great cities, pull a dish of stewed oysters close to her, and with a table-spoon fish out and eat the oysters one at a time; audibly sipping up their liquor from the said dish.

We have seen a young *gentleman* lift his plate of soup in both hands, hold it to his mouth and drink, or rather lap it up.

Some persons behave coarsely at a public table because they are ignorant, and know no better. Some (far less excusable) are rude because they are too selfish to put any restraint on their inclinations, or to care for the convenience of others.

Some display, all the time, a vulgar determination to "get the full worth of their money." Some, who at a *private* dinner-table would be the most polite people imaginable, lay aside their good manners in a *public* dining-room; regarding a hotel as they would a tavern—a sort of Liberty Hall.

Chapter X

LETTERS

PARCHMENT AND POSTAGE

In writing upon business exclusively your own, for instance to make a request, to ask for information, to petition for a favour, or to solicit an autograph, it is but right not only to pay the postage of your own letter, but to enclose a stamp for the answer. This is always done by really polite and considerate people. You have no right, when the benefit is entirely your own, to cause any extra expense to the receiver of the letter—not even the cost of three cents to pay the postage back again. It is enough to tax their time by requiring them to write to you and send off the reply. Also, in corresponding with a relative, or very intimate friend, to whom even a small expense is of more importance than to yourself, you may enclose a stamp for the answer. Do so always in writing to poor people. Be careful not to allow yourself to get entirely out of post-office stamps. Replenish your stock in time. If the gum on the back seems too weak, go over it afresh with that excellent cement, "Perpetual Paste." Embossed or bordered envelopes are not often used except in notes of ceremony—or when the acquaintance is slight. The same with ornamented note-paper. Intimate friends and relatives use paper that is handsome, but plain. Letters of business are generally enclosed in yellow or buff-coloured envelopes. Some of these yellow envelopes are large enough to contain a folio sheet when folded. Notes *not* to be sent by post, are usually sealed with wax—the seal very small. But a *small* wafer is admissible—a white one looks best for a note. In folding your note or letter, see that it is not too large to go into the envelope. It is customary to write the direction on the envelope only. Nevertheless, if the letter is to go a long distance by post, the envelope may be worn off, or torn off accidentally, or get so damaged in the letter-bag as to be rendered illegible. The surest and safest way is to put the address on the letter also; or if the sheet is full, to find a corner for the direction, either at the beginning or end.

In paper, as in most other things, the best is the cheapest. If the tint is bluish, the writing will not be so legible as on a pure white. The surface should be smooth and glossy. For letter writing *ruled* paper is rarely used, except by children. In writing for the press, no other is so convenient. A page of ruled lines to slip beneath, is indispensable to those who cannot otherwise write straight.

THE FORMALITIES OF LETTER-WRITING

If you are addressing a friend and have much to say, and expect to fill the sheet, begin very near the top of the first page. But if your letter is to be a short one, commence lower down, several inches from the top. If a *very* short letter of only a few lines, begin but a little above the middle of the page. Crossing a letter all over with transverse lines is obsolete. It is intolerable to read, and there is no excuse for it now, when postage is so low, and every body pays their own.

Write the date near the right-hand side of the first page, and place it about two lines higher than the two or three words of greeting or accosting with which letters usually commence. Begin the first sentence a little below those words, and farther toward the right than the lines that are to follow. It is well in dating *every* letter to give always your exact residence—that is, not only the town you live in, but the number and street. If your correspondent has had *but one* notification of your present place of abode, she may have forgotten the number, and even the street. Your letter containing it may not be at hand as a reference, and the answer may, in consequence, be misdirected—or directed in so vague a manner that it will never reach you. We have known much inconvenience (and indeed loss) ensue from not specifying with the date of *each* letter the exact dwelling-place of the writer. But if it is *always* indicated at the top of *every one*, a reference to *any* one of your letters will furnish your proper address. If you are in the country, where there are no streets or numbered houses, give the name of the estate and that of the nearest post-town; also the county and state. All this will occupy a long line, but you will find the advantage. If your letter fills more than one sheet, number each page. Should you have no envelope, leave, on the inside of the third page, two blank spaces where the seal is to come. These spaces should be left rather too large than too small. Lest you should tear the letter in *breaking* it open, it is best to *cut* round the seal. We have seen letters that were actually illegible from the paleness of the ink. If you write from your own house this is inexcusable, as you ought always to be *well* supplied with that indispensable article; and in a city you can easily send to a stationer's and buy it.

If you make a mistake in a word, draw your pen through it, or score it so as to be quite illegible, and then interline the correction, placing a caret beneath. This will be better than scratching out the error with your penknife, and afterward trying to write a new word in the identical place; an attempt which rarely succeeds, even with the aid of pounce-powder, which is pulverised gum-sandarac.

SIGNED, SEALED, DELIVERED

At the end of the letter, somewhat lower than your signature, (which should be very near the right-hand edge of the page,) add the name and address of the person for whom the letter is designed, and to whom it will thus find its way, even if the envelope should be defaced, or torn off and lost. Write your own name rather larger than your usual hand, and put a dot or dash after it.

For sealing letters no light is so convenient as a wax taper in a low stand. A lamp, or candle, may smoke or blacken the wax. To seal well, your wax should be of the finest quality. Red wax of a bright scarlet colour is the best. Low-priced wax consumes very fast; and when melted, looks purplish or brownish. When going to melt sealing-wax, rest your elbow on the table to keep your hand steady. Take the stick of wax between your thumb and finger, and hold it a little above the light, so that it barely touches the point of the flame. Turn the stick round till it is equally softened on all sides. Then insert a little of the melted wax *under* the turn-over part of the letter, just where the seal is to come. This will render it more secure than if the sole dependence was on the outside seal. Or instead of this little touch of wax, you may slip beneath the turn-over a small wafer, either white or of the same colour as the wax. Then begin at the outer edge of the place you intend for the seal; and move the wax in a circle, which must gradually diminish till it terminates in the centre. Put the seal exactly to the middle of the soft wax, and press it down hard, but do not screw it round. Then withdraw it suddenly. Do not use motto seals unless writing to a member of your own family, or to an intimate friend. For common service, (and particularly for letters of business,) a plain seal, with simply your initials, is best.

For a note always use a very small seal. In addressing one of your own family, it is not necessary to follow scrupulously all these observances. In writing to persons decidedly your inferiors in station, avoid the probability of mortifying them by sending mean, ill-looking notes.

A TIP FROM THE AUTHOR

Remember also (what, strange to say, some people calling themselves ladies seem not to know) that a note commenced in the first person must continue in the first person all through. The same when it begins in the third person. We have heard of invitations to a party being worded thus:—

Mrs. Welford's compliments to Mrs. Marley, and requests the pleasure of her company on Thursday evening.
Yours sincerely,
E. Welford

WRITING INVITATIONS AND RSVPS

Notes of invitation should always designate both the day of the week and that of the month. If that of *the month only* is specified, one figure may perhaps be mistaken for another; for instance, the 13th may look like the 18th, or the 25th like the 26th. We know instances where, from this cause, some of the guests did not come till the night *after* the party.

There are some very sensible people who, in their invitations, tell frankly what is to be expected, and if they really ask but *a few* friends, they at once give the names of those friends, so that you may know whom you are to see. If you are to meet no more than can sit round the tea-table, they signify the same. If they expect twenty, thirty, or forty persons, they say so—and do not leave you in doubt whether to dress for something very like a party, or for a mere family tea-drinking.

If it is a decided music-party, by all means specify the same, that those who have no enjoyment of what is considered fashionable music, may stay away.

Always reply to a note of invitation the day after you have received it. To a note on business send an answer the same day. After accepting an invitation, should any thing occur to prevent your going, send a second note in due time.

Do not take offence at a friend because she does not invite you every time she has company. Her regard for you may be as warm as ever, but it is probably inconvenient for her to have more than a certain number at a time.

Believe that the omission is no evidence of neglect, or of a desire to offend you; but rest assured that you are to be invited on other occasions. If you are *not*, then indeed you may take it as a hint that she is no longer desirous of continuing the acquaintance. Be dignified enough not to call her to account; but cease visiting her, without taking her to task and bringing on a quarrel. But if you *must* quarrel, let it not be in writing. A paper war is always carried too far, and produces bitterness of feeling which is seldom entirely eradicated, even after apologies have been made and accepted. Still, when an offence has been given in writing, the atonement should be made in writing also.

ONE LETTER TOO MANY

Much time is wasted (particularly by young ladies) in writing and answering such epistles as are termed "letters of friendship,"—meaning long documents (frequently with crossed lines) filled with regrets at absence, asseverations of eternal affection, modest deprecations of your humble self, and enthusiastic glorifyings of your exalted correspondent; or else wonderments at both of you being so much alike, and so very congenial; and anticipations of rapture at meeting again, and lamentations at the slow progress of time, till the exact hour of re-union shall arrive—the *postscript* usually containing some confidential allusion to a lover, (either real or supposed,) and perhaps a kind enquiry about a real or supposed lover of your friend's.

Now such letters as these are of no manner of use but to foster a sickly, morbid feeling, (very often a fictitious one,) and to encourage nonsense, and destroy all relish for such true friendship as is good and wholesome.

A still worse species of voluminous female correspondence is that which turns *entirely* upon love, or rather on what are called "beaux;" or entirely on hate—for instance, hatred of step-mothers. This topic is considered the more *piquant* from its impropriety, and from its being carried on in secret.

Then there are young ladies born with the organ of letter-writing amazingly developed, and increased by perpetual practice, who can scarcely become acquainted with a gentleman possessing brains, without volunteering a correspondence with him. And then ensues a long epistolary dialogue about nothing, or at least nothing worth reading or remembering; trenching closely on gallantry, but still not quite *that*; affected flippancy on the part of the lady; and unaffected impertinence on that of the gentleman, "which serves her right"—alternating with pretended poutings on her side, and half or whole-laughing apologies on his. Sometimes there are attempts at moralising, or criticising, or sentimentalising— but nothing is ever elicited that, to a third person, can afford the least amusement or improvement, or excite the least interest. Yet, strange to say, gentlemen have been inveigled into this sort of correspondence, even by ladies who have made a business of afterward selling the letters for publication, and making money out of them. And such epistles have actually been printed. We do not suppose they have been read. The public is very stubborn in refusing to read what neither amuses, interests, or improves—even when a publisher is actually so weak as to print such things.

No young lady ever engages in a correspondence with a gentleman that is neither her relative or her betrothed, without eventually lessening herself in his eyes. Of this she may rest assured. With some men, it is even dangerous for a lady to write a note on the commonest subject. He may show the superscription, or the signature, or both, to his idle companions, and make insinuations much to her disadvantage, which his comrades will be sure to circulate and exaggerate.

Above all, let no lady correspond with a married man, unless she is obliged to consult him on business; and from that plain, straight path let her not diverge. Even if the wife sees and reads every letter, she will, in all probability, feel a touch of jealousy, (or more than a touch,) if she finds that they excite interest in her husband, or give him pleasure. This will inevitably be the case if the married lady is inferior in intellect to the single one, and has a lurking consciousness that she is so.

DOTTING THE 'I'S AND CROSSING THE 'T'S

Having hinted what the correspondence of young ladies ought *not* to be, we will try to convey some idea of what it ought. Let us premise that there is no danger of *any* errors in grammar or spelling, and but few faults of punctuation, and that the fair writers are aware that a sentence should always conclude with a period or full stop, to be followed by a capital letter beginning the next sentence; and that a new paragraph should be allotted to every change of subject, provided that there is room on the sheet of paper. And still, it is well to have always at hand a dictionary and a grammar, in case of unaccountable lapses of memory. However, persons who have read much, and read to advantage, generally find themselves at no loss in orthography, grammar, and punctuation. To spell badly is disgraceful in a lady or gentleman, and it looks as if they had quitted reading as soon as they quitted school.

To write a legible and handsome hand is an accomplishment not sufficiently valued. And yet of what importance it is! We are always vexed when we hear people of talent making a sort of boast of the illegibility of their writing, and relating anecdotes of the difficulty with which it has been read, and the mistakes made by its decipherers. There are persons who affect bad writing, and boast of it, because the worst signatures extant are those of Shakespeare, Bonaparte, and Byron. These men were great in spite of their autographs, not because of them.

Read over each page of your letter, as you finish it, to see that there are no errors. If you find any, correct them carefully. In writing a familiar letter, a very common fault is tautology, or a too frequent repetition of the same word—for instance, "Yesterday I received a letter from sister Mary, which was the first letter I have received from sister since she left." The sentence should be, "Yesterday I received a letter from my sister Mary, the first since she left us."

Unless you are writing to one of your own family, put always the pronoun "*my*" before the word "sister."

Say also—"my father," "my mother," and not "father," "mother," as if they were also the parents of your correspondent.

To end the sentence with the word "left," (for departed,) is awkward and unsatisfactory—for instance, "It is two days since he left." Left what? It is one of the absurd innovations that have crept in among us of late years, and are supposed to be fashionable. Another is the ridiculous way of omitting the possessive S in words ending with that letter; for instance, "Sims' Hotel" instead of "Sims's Hotel"—"Jenkins' Bakery" for "Jenkins's Bakery." Would any one, in talking, say they had stayed at Sims' Hotel, or that they bought their bread at Jenkins' Bakery. This is ungrammatical, as it obliterates the possessive case, and is therefore indefinite; and moreover, it looks and sounds awkwardly.

Many persons who think themselves good grammarians put on their cards "The Misses Brown,"— "The Misses Smith." Those who *really* are so, write "The Miss Browns"—"The Miss Smiths"—the plural being always on the substantive, and never on the adjective. Would we say "the whites glove" instead of "the white gloves"—or the "blues ribbon" for the "blue ribbons." Does any lady in talking say, "The two Misses Brown called to see me?"

It is also wrong to say "two *spoons*ful," instead of two *spoon*fuls. Thus, "two spoonsful of milk" seems to imply two separate spoons with milk in each; while "two spoonfuls of milk" gives the true idea—one spoon twice filled.

WRITING IN AN APPROPRIATE MANNER

Avoid in writing, as in talking, all words that do not express the true meaning. We are sorry to say that sometimes even among educated people, when attempting smartness or wit, we find a sort of conventional slang that has, in truth, a strong tinge of vulgarity, being the wilful substitution of bad words or bad phrases for good ones. When we find them issuing from the lips or the pen of a *lady*, we fear she is unfortunate in a reprobate husband, or brother, from whom she must have learnt them. Yet even reprobates dislike to hear their wives and sisters talking coarsely.

Unless you know that your correspondent is well versed in French, refrain from interlarding your letters with Gallic words or phrases.

Do not introduce long quotations from poetry. Three or four lines of verse are sufficient. One line, or two, are better still. Write them rather smaller than your usual hand, and leave a space at the beginning and end; marking their commencement and termination with inverted commas, thus " ".

SECRETS AND SNOOPING

To break the seal of a letter directed to another person is punishable by law. To read *secretly* the letter of another is morally as felonious. A woman who would act thus meanly is worse than those who apply their eyes or ears to key-holes, or door-cracks, or who listen under windows, or look down from attics upon their neighbours; or who, in a dusky parlour, before the lamps are lighted, ensconce themselves in a corner, and give no note of their presence while listening to a conversation not intended for them to hear.

We do not conceive that, unless he authorises her to do so, (which he had best not,) a wife is justifiable in opening her husband's letters, or he in reading hers. Neither wife nor husband has any right to entrust to the other the secrets of their friends; and letters may contain such secrets. Unless under extraordinary circumstances, parents should not consider themselves privileged to inspect the correspondence of grown-up children. Brothers and sisters always take care that their epistles shall not be unceremoniously opened by each other. In short, a letter is the property of the person to whom it is addressed, and nobody has a right to read it without permission.

If you are shown an autograph signature at the bottom of a letter, be satisfied to look at *that only*; and do not open out, and read the whole—unless desired.

Chapter XI

PRESENTS

OBLIGATIONS OF THE RECEIVER

Having accepted a present, it is your duty, and ought to be your pleasure, to let the giver see that you make use of it as intended, and that it is not thrown away upon you. If it is an article of dress, or of personal decoration, take occasion, on the first *suitable* opportunity, to wear it in presence of the giver. If an ornament for the centre-table, or the mantel-piece, place it there. If a book, do not delay reading it. Afterward, speak of it to her as favourably as you can. If of fruit or flowers, refer to them the next time you see her.

In all cases, when a gift is sent to you, return a note of thanks; or at least a verbal message to that effect.

Never enquire of the giver what was the price of her gift, or where she bought it. To do so is considered exceedingly rude.

When an article is presented to you for a specified purpose, it is your duty to use it for *that* purpose, and for no other, according to the wish of the donor. It is mean and dishonourable to give away a present; at least without first obtaining permission from the original giver. You have no right to be liberal or generous at the expense of another, or to accept a gift with a secret determination to bestow it *yourself* on somebody else. If it is an article that you do not want, that you possess already, or that you cannot use for yourself, it is best to say so candidly, at once; expressing your thanks for the offer, and requesting your friend to keep it for some other person to whom it will be advantageous. It is fit that the purchaser of the gift should have the pleasure of doing a kindness with her own hand, and eliciting the gratitude of one whom she knows herself. It is paltry in you to deprive her of this pleasure, by first accepting a present, and then secretly giving it away as from yourself.

There are instances of women whose circumstances did not allow them to indulge often in delicacies, that on a present of early fruit, or some other nice thing being sent to them by a kind friend, have ostentatiously transferred the gift to a wealthy neighbour, with a view of having it supposed that they had bought it themselves, and that to *them* such things were no rarities. This is contemptible—but it is sometimes done.

LIMITATIONS OF THE GIVER

Making a valuable present to a rich person is in most cases, a work of supererogation; unless the gift is of something rare or *unique*, which cannot be purchased, and which may be seen and used to more advantage at the house of your friend than while in your own possession. But to give an expensive article of dress, jewellery, or furniture to one whose means of buying such things are quite equal (if not superior) to your own, is an absurdity; though not a very uncommon one, as society is now constituted. Such gifts elicit no real gratitude, for in all probability, they may not suit the pampered taste of those to whom fine things are no novelties. Or they may be regarded (however unjustly) as baits or nets to catch, in return, something of still greater cost.

There are persons, who, believing that presents are generally made with some mercenary view, and being unwilling themselves to receive favours, or incur obligations, make a point of repaying them as soon as possible, by a gift of something equivalent. This at once implies that they suspect the motive. If sincere in her friendship, the donor of the first present will feel hurt at being directly paid for it, and consider that she has been treated rudely, and unjustly. On the other hand, if compensation *was* secretly desired, and really expected, she will be disappointed at receiving nothing in return. Therefore, we repeat, that among persons who can conveniently provide themselves with whatever they may desire, the bestowal of presents is generally a most unthankful business. If you are in opulent circumstances, it is best to limit your generosity to such friends only as do not abound in the gifts of fortune, and whose situation denies them the means of indulging their tastes. By them such acts of kindness will be duly appreciated, and gratefully remembered; and the article presented will have a double value, if it is to them a novelty.

GIFTS FOR SPECIAL OCCASIONS

Gratitude is a very pleasant sensation, both for those who feel and to those who excite it. No one who confers a favour can say *with truth*, that "they want no thanks." They always do.

We know not why, when a young lady of fortune is going to be married, her friends should all be expected to present her with bridal gifts. It is a custom that sometimes bears heavily on those whose condition allows them but little to spare. And from that little it may be very hard for them to squeeze out enough to purchase some superfluous ornament, or some bauble for a centre-table, when it is already glittering with the gifts of the opulent;—gifts lavished on one who is really in no need of such things; and whose marriage confers no benefit on any one but herself. Why should she be rewarded for gratifying her own inclination in marrying the man of her choice? Now that it is fashionable to display all the wedding-gifts arranged in due form on tables, and labelled with the names of the donors, the seeming necessity of giving something expensive, or at least elegant, has become more onerous than ever. What we contend is, that on a marriage in a wealthy family, the making of presents should be confined to the immediate relatives of the lady, and only to such of *them* as can well afford it.

At christenings, it is fortunately the sponsors only that are expected to make gifts to the infant. Therefore, invite no persons as sponsors, who cannot well afford this expense; unless you are sufficiently intimate to request them, privately, not to comply with the custom; being unwilling that they should cause themselves inconvenience by doing so.

The presentation of Christmas and New-Year's gifts is often a severe tax on persons with whom money is not plenty. It would be well if it were the universal custom to expect and receive no presents from any but the rich.

GIFTS FOR CHILDREN

In making gifts to children, choose for them only such things as will afford them somewhat of lasting amusement. For boys, kites, tops, balls, marbles, wheelbarrows, carts, gardening utensils, and carpenter's tools, &c. Showy toys, that are merely to look at, and from which they can derive no enjoyment but in breaking them to pieces, are not worth buying. Little girls delight in little tea-sets, and dinner-sets, in which they can "make feasts," miniature kitchen-utensils, to play at cooking, washing, &c.; and dolls so dressed that all the clothes can be taken off and put on at pleasure. They soon grow tired of a doll whose glittering habiliments are sewed fast upon her. A wax doll in elegant attire is too precarious and expensive a plaything to make them happy; as they are always afraid of injuring her.

To an intelligent child, no gifts are so valuable as entertaining books—provided they really *are* entertaining. Children are generally wise enough to prefer an amusing book in a plain cover, to a dull one shining with gold. When children are able to read fluently, they lose much of their desire for mere picture-books. If the cuts are badly executed, and give ugly, disagreeable ideas of the characters in the stories, they only trouble and annoy the little readers, instead of pleasing them.

Children have less enjoyment than is supposed in being taken to shops to choose gifts for themselves, or even in laying out their own money. It is always a long time before they can decide on what to buy, and as soon as they have fixed upon one thing, they immediately see something they like better. And often, after getting home, they are dissatisfied with their choice, and sorry they bought it. Also, they frequently wear out the patience of the shopkeepers; being desirous of seeing every thing, and pondering so long before they can determine on buying any thing.

It is every way better to go to the shops without them, buy what you think proper, and then give them an agreeable surprise by the presentation.

ACCEPTING GIFTS FROM MEN

Young ladies should be careful how they accept presents from gentlemen. No truly modest and dignified woman will incur such obligations. And no gentleman who really respects her will offer her any thing more than a bouquet, a book, one or two autographs of distinguished persons, or a few relics or mementos of memorable places— things that derive their chief value from associations. But to present a young lady with articles of jewellery, or of dress, or with a costly ornament for the centre-table, (unless she is his affianced wife,) ought to be regarded as an offence, rather than a compliment, excusable only in a man sadly ignorant of the refinements of society. And if he is so, she should set him right, and civilly, but firmly, refuse to be his debtor.

Yet, we are sorry to say, that there are ladies so rapacious, and so mean, that they are not ashamed to give broad hints to gentlemen, (particularly those gentlemen who are either very young or very old,) regarding certain beautiful card-cases, bracelets, essence-bottles, &c. which they have seen and admired,—even going so far as to fall in love with elegant shawls, scarfs, splendid fans, and embroidered handkerchiefs. And their admiration is so violent, and so reiterated, that the gentleman knows not how to resist; he therefore puts them in possession of a gift far too costly for any woman of delicacy to accept. In such cases, the father or mother of the young lady should oblige her to return the present. This has been done.

There are ladies who keep themselves supplied with certain articles of finery, (for instance, white kid gloves,) by laying ridiculous wagers with gentlemen, knowing that, whether winning or losing, the gentleman, out of gallantry, always pays. No lady should ever lay wagers, even with one of her own sex. It is foolish and unfeminine—and no man likes her any the better for indulging in the practice.

Some young ladies, who profess a sort of daughterly regard for certain wealthy old gentlemen, are so kind as to knit purses or work slippers for them, or some other nick-nacks, (provided always that the "dear old man" has a character for generosity,) for they know that he will reward them by a handsome present of some bijou of real value. And yet they may be assured that the kind old gentleman (whom "they mind no more than if he was their pa") sees through the whole plan, knows why the purse was knit, or the slippers worked, and esteems the kind young lady accordingly.

Another, and highly reprehensible way of extorting a gift, is to have what is called a philopena with a gentleman. This very silly joke is when a young lady, in cracking almonds, chances to find two kernels in one shell; she shares them with a beau; which ever first calls out "*philopena*," on their next meeting, is entitled to receive a present from the other; and she is to remind him of it till he remembers to comply. So much nonsense is often talked on the occasion, that it seems to expand into something of importance; and the gentleman thinks he can do no less, than purchase for the lady something very elegant, or valuable; particularly if he has heard her tell of the munificence of other beaux in their philopenas.

There is great want of delicacy and self-respect in philopenaism, and no lady who has a proper sense of her dignity *as a lady* will engage in any thing of the sort.

A HELPING HAND

In presenting a dress to a friend whose circumstances are not so affluent as your own, and who you know will gladly receive it, select one of excellent quality, and of a colour that you think she will like. She will feel mortified, if you give her one that is low-priced, flimsy, and of an unbecoming tint. Get an ample quantity, so as to allow a piece to be cut off and laid by for a new body and sleeves, when necessary. And to make the gift complete, buy linen for the body-lining; stiff, glazed muslin for the facings; buttons, sewing-silk, and whatever else may be wanted. This will save her the cost of these things.

When you give a dress to a poor woman, it is far better to buy for her a substantial new one, than to bestow on her an old thin gown of your own. The poor have little leisure to sew for themselves; and second-hand fine clothes last them but a very short time before they are fit only for the rag-bag.

If you are going to have a party, and among your very *intimate* friends is one whose circumstances will not permit her to incur the expense of buying a handsome new dress for the occasion, and if she has no choice but to stay away, or to appear in a costume very inferior to that of the other ladies, you may (if you can well afford it) obviate this difficulty by presenting her with a proper dress-pattern, and other accessories. This may be managed anonymously, but it will be better to do it with her knowledge. It will be a very gratifying mark of your friendship; and she ought to consider it as such, and not refuse it from a feeling of false pride. Of course, it will be kept a secret from all but yourselves. In the overflow of gratitude *she* may speak of it to others, but for *you* to mention it would be ungenerous and indelicate in the extreme. We are glad to say that ladies of fortune often make gifts of party-dresses to their less-favoured friends.

A TIP FROM THE AUTHOR

In sending a present, always pay in advance the expense of transmitting it, so that it may cost nothing at all to the receiver. You may send by the Mail a package of any size, weighing not more than four pounds, paying the postage yourself at the office from whence it goes. It will then be delivered at the door of your friend, without further charge.

Chapter XII

CONVERSATION

A BRIEF SUMMARY

Conversation is the verbal interchange of thoughts and feelings. To form a *perfect* conversationist, many qualifications are requisite. There must be knowledge of the world, knowledge of books, and a facility of imparting that knowledge; together with originality, memory, an intuitive perception of what is best to say, and best to omit, good taste, good temper, and good manners. An agreeable and instructive talker has the faculty of going "from gay to grave, from lively to serene," without any apparent effort; neither skimming so slightly over a variety of topics as to leave no impression of any, or dwelling so long upon one subject as to weary the attention of the hearers. Persons labouring under a monomania, such as absorbs their whole mind into one prevailing idea, are never pleasant or impressive talkers. They defeat their own purpose by recurring to it perpetually, and rendering it a perpetual fatigue. A good talker should cultivate a temperance in talking; so as not to talk too much, to the exclusion of other good talkers. Conversation is dialogue, not monologue.

To be a perfect conversationist, a good voice is indispensable—a voice that is clear, distinct, and silver-toned. If you find that you have a habit of speaking too low, "reform it altogether." It is a bad one; and will render your talk unintelligible.

AGREEABLE ACQUAINTANCES, AGREEABLE CONVERSATION

Few things are more delightful than for one intelligent and well-stored mind to find itself in company with a kindred spirit—each understanding the other, catching every idea, and comprehending every allusion. Such persons will become as intimate in half an hour, as if they had been personally acquainted for years.

On the other hand, the pleasure of society is much lessened by the habit in which many persons indulge, of placing themselves always in the opposition, controverting every opinion, and doubting every fact. They talk to you as a lawyer examines a witness at the bar; trying to catch you in some discrepancy that will invalidate your testimony; fixing their scrutinising eyes upon your face "as if they would look you through," and scarcely permitting you to say, "It is a fine day," without making you prove your words. Such people are never popular. Nobody likes perpetual contradiction, especially when the subject of argument is of little or no consequence. In young people this dogmatic practice is generally based upon vanity and impertinence. In the old it is prompted by pride and selfishness.

LET US TALK BUSINESS, OR NOT

Unless he first refers to it himself, never talk to a gentleman concerning his profession; at least do not question him about it. For instance, you must not expect a physician to tell you how his patients are affected, or to confide to you any particulars of their maladies. These are subjects that he will discuss only with their relatives, or their nurses. It is also very improper to ask a lawyer about his clients, or the cases in which he is employed. A clergyman does not like always to be talking about the church. A merchant, when away from his counting-house, has no wish to engage in business-talk with ladies; and a mechanic is ever willing "to leave the shop behind him." Still, there are some few individuals who like to talk of their bread-winner. If you perceive this disposition, indulge them, and listen attentively. You will learn something useful, and worth remembering.

Women who have begun the world in humble life, and have been necessitated to give most of their attention to household affairs, are generally very shy in talking of housewifery, after their husbands have become rich, and are living in style, as it is called. Therefore, do not annoy them by questions on domestic economy. But converse as if they had been ladies always.

FOR RICHER, FOR POORER

Never remind any one of the time when their situation was less genteel, or less affluent than at present, or tell them that you remember their living in a small house, or in a remote street. If they have not moral courage to talk of such things themselves, it is rude in you to make any allusion to them.

On the other hand, if invited to a fashionable house, and to meet fashionable company, it is not the time or place for you to set forth the comparative obscurity of your own origin, by way of showing that you are not proud. If *you* are not proud, it is most likely that your entertainers may be, and they will not be pleased at your ultra-magnanimity in thus lowering yourself before their aristocratic guests. These communications should be reserved for *tête-à-têtes* with old or familiar friends, who have no more pride than yourself.

DOUBTS AND DECEIT

When listening to a circumstance that is stated to have actually occurred to the relater, even if it strikes you as being very extraordinary, and not in conformity to your own experience, it is rude to reply, "Such a thing never happened to *me*." It is rude because it seems to imply a doubt of the narrator's veracity; and it is foolish, because its not having happened to *you* is no proof that it could not have happened to any body else. Slowness in belief is sometimes an evidence of ignorance, rather than of knowledge. People who have read but little, travelled but little, and seen but little of the world out of their own immediate circle, and whose intellect is too obtuse to desire any new accession to their own small stock of ideas, are apt to think that nothing can be true unless it has fallen under their own limited experience. Also, they may be so circumstanced that nothing in the least out of the common way is likely to disturb the still water of their pond-like existence.

When you hear a gentleman speak in praise of a lady whom you do not think deserving of his commendations, you will gain nothing by attempting to undeceive him; particularly if she is handsome. Your dissenting from his opinion he will, in all probability, impute to envy, or ill-nature; and therefore the only impression you can make will be against yourself.

Even if you have reason to dislike the lady, recollect that few are without some good points both of person and character. And it will be much better for you to pass over her faults in silence, and agree with him in commending what is really commendable about her. What he would, perhaps, believe implicitly if told to him by a man, he would attribute entirely to jealousy, or to a love of detraction if related by a woman. Above all, if a gentleman descants on the beauty of a lady, and in your own mind you do not coincide with his opinion, refrain, on your part, from criticising invidiously her face and figure, and do not say that "though her complexion may be fine, her features are not regular;" that "her nose is too small," or "her eyes too large," or "her mouth too wide." Still less disclose to him the secret of her wearing false hair, artificial teeth, or tinging her cheeks with rouge. If she is a bold, forward woman, he will find that out as soon as yourself, and sooner too,—and you may be sure that though he may amuse himself by talking and flirting with her, he in reality regards her as she deserves.

A TIP FROM THE AUTHOR

If a foreigner chances, in your presence, to make an unfavourable remark upon some custom or habit peculiar to your country, do not immediately take fire and resent it; for, perhaps, upon reflection, you may find that he is right, or nearly so. All countries have their national character, and no character is perfect, whether that of a nation or an individual. If you know that the stranger has imbibed an erroneous impression, you may calmly, and in a few words, endeavour to convince him of it.

BROACHING CONTROVERSIAL SUBJECTS

It is very unmannerly when a person begins to relate a circumstance or an anecdote, to stop them short by saying, "I have heard it before." Still worse, to say you do not wish to hear it at all. There are people who set themselves against listening to any thing that can possibly excite melancholy or painful feelings; and profess to hear nothing that may give them a sad or unpleasant sensation. Those who have so much tenderness for themselves, have usually but little tenderness for others. It is impossible to go through the world with perpetual sunshine over head, and unfading flowers under foot. Clouds will gather in the brightest sky, and weeds choke up the fairest primroses and violets. And we should all endeavour to prepare ourselves for these changes, by listening with sympathy to the manner in which they have affected others.

No person of good feelings, good manners, or true refinement, will entertain their friends with minute descriptions of sickening horrors, such as barbarous executions, revolting punishments, or inhuman cruelties perpetrated on animals. We have never heard an officer dilate on the dreadful spectacle of a battlefield; a scene of which no description can ever present an adequate idea; and which no painter has ever exhibited in all its shocking and disgusting details. Physicians do not talk of the dissecting-room.

Unless you are speaking to a physician, and are interested in a patient he is attending, refrain in conversation from entering into the particulars of revolting diseases, such as scrofula, ulcers, cutaneous afflictions, &c. and discuss no terrible operations—especially at table. There are women who seem to delight in dwelling on such disagreeable topics.

If you are attending the sick-bed of a friend, and are called down to a visiter, speak of her illness with delicacy, and do not disclose all the unpleasant circumstances connected with it; things which it would grieve her to know, may, if once told, be circulated among married women, and by them repeated to their husbands. In truth, upon most occasions, a married woman is not a safe confidant. She will assuredly tell every thing to her husband; and in all probability to his mother and sisters also—that is, every thing concerning her friends—always, perhaps, under a strict injunction of secrecy. But a secret entrusted to more than two or three persons, is soon diffused throughout the whole community.

A MAN'S WORLD

Generally speaking, it is injudicious for ladies to attempt arguing with gentlemen on political or financial topics. All the information that a woman can possibly acquire or remember on these subjects is so small, in comparison with the knowledge of men, that the discussion will not elevate them in the opinion of masculine minds. Still, it is well for a woman to desire enlightenment, that she may comprehend something of these discussions, when she hears them from the other sex; therefore let her listen as understandingly as she can, but refrain from controversy and argument on such topics as the grasp of a female mind is seldom capable of seizing or retaining. Men are very intolerant toward women who are prone to contradiction and contention, when the talk is of things considered out of their sphere; but very indulgent toward a modest and attentive listener, who only asks questions for the sake of information. Men like to dispense knowledge; but few of them believe that in departments exclusively their own, they can profit much by the suggestions of women.

RELIGIOUS MUSINGS

In talking with a stranger, if the conversation should turn toward sectarian religion, enquire to what church he belongs; and then mention your own church. This, among people of good sense and good manners, and we may add of true piety, will preclude all danger of remarks being made on either side which may be painful to either party. Happily we live in a land of universal toleration, where all religions are equal in the sight of the law and the government; and where no text is more powerful and more universally received than the wise and incontrovertible words—"By their fruits ye shall know them." He that acts well is a good man, and a religious man, at whatever altar he may worship. He that acts ill is a bad man, and has no true sense of religion; no matter how punctual his attendance at church, if of that church he is an unworthy member. Ostentatious sanctimony may deceive man, but it cannot deceive God.

HAVE AN OPINION, BUT MAKE IT THE RIGHT ONE

In giving your opinion of a new book, a picture, or a piece of music, when conversing with a distinguished author, an artist or a musician, say modestly, that "so it appears to *you*"—that "it has given *you* pleasure," or the contrary. But do not positively and dogmatically assert that it *is* good, or that it *is* bad. The person with whom you are talking is, in all probability, a far more competent judge than yourself; therefore, listen attentively, and he may correct your opinion, and set you right. If he fails to convince you, remain silent, or change the subject. Vulgar ladies have often a way of saying, when disputing on the merits of a thing they are incapable of understanding, "Any how, *I* like it," or, "It is quite good enough for *me*."—Which is no proof of its being good enough for any body else.

GOSSIPERS

In being asked your candid opinion of a person, be very cautious to whom you confide that opinion; for if repeated as yours, it may lead to unpleasant consequences. It is only to an intimate and long-tried friend that you may safely entrust certain things, which if known, might produce mischief. Even very intimate friends are not always to be trusted, and when they have actually told something that they heard under the injunction of secrecy, they will consider it a sufficient atonement to say, "Indeed I did not mean to tell it, but somehow it slipped out;" or, "I really intended to guard the secret faithfully, but I was so questioned and cross-examined, and bewildered, that I knew not how to answer without disclosing enough to make them guess the whole. I am very sorry, and will try to be more cautious in future. But these slips of the tongue will happen."

The lady whose confidence has been thus betrayed, should be "more cautious in future," and put no farther trust in she of the slippery tongue—giving her up, entirely, as unworthy of farther friendship.

No circumstances will induce an honourable and right-minded woman to reveal a secret after promising secrecy. But she should refuse being made the depository of any extraordinary fact which it may be wrong to conceal, and wrong to disclose.

We can scarcely find words sufficiently strong to contemn the heinous practice, so prevalent with low-minded people, of repeating to their friends whatever they hear to their disadvantage. By low-minded people, we do not exclusively mean persons of low station. The low-minded are not always "born in a garret, in a kitchen bred." Unhappily, there are (so-called) ladies—ladies of fortune and fashion—who will descend to meannesses of which the higher ranks ought to be considered incapable, and who, without compunction, will wantonly lacerate the feelings and mortify the self-love of those whom they call their friends, telling them what has been said about them by other friends.

It is sometimes said of a notorious tatler and mischief-maker, that "she has, notwithstanding, a good heart." How is this possible, when it is her pastime to scatter dissension, ill-feeling, and unhappiness among all whom she calls her friends? She may, perhaps, give alms to beggars, or belong to sewing circles, or to Bible societies, or be officious in visiting the sick. All this is meritorious, and it is well if there is some good in her. But if she violates the charities of social life, and takes a malignant pleasure in giving pain, and causing trouble—depend on it, her show of benevolence is mere ostentation, and her acts of kindness spring not from the heart. She will convert the sewing circle into a scandal circle. If she is assiduous in visiting her sick friends, she will turn to the worst account, particulars she may thus acquire of the sanctities of private life and the humiliating mysteries of the sick-chamber.

If indeed it can be possible that tatling and mischief-making may be only (as is sometimes alleged) a bad habit, proceeding from an inability to govern the tongue—

shame on those who have allowed themselves to acquire such a habit, and who make no effort to subdue it, or who have encouraged it in their children, and perhaps set them the example.

If you are so unfortunate as to know one of these pests of society, get rid of her acquaintance as soon as you can.

DEALING WITH CRITICISMS AND ILL-TEMPERED PEOPLE

If a person begins by telling you, "Do not be offended at what I am going to say," prepare yourself for something that she knows will certainly offend you. But as she has given you notice, try to listen, and answer with calmness.

It is a delicate and thankless business to tell a friend of her faults, unless you are certain that, in return, you can bear without anger to hear her point out your own. She will undoubtedly recriminate.

It is not true that an irritable temper cannot be controlled. It can, and is, whenever the worldly interest of the *enragée* depends on its suppression.

Frederick the Great severely reprimanded a Prussian officer for striking a soldier at a review. "I could not refrain," said the officer. "I have a high temper, your majesty, and I cannot avoid showing it, when I see a man looking sternly at me." "Yes, you can," replied the king. "I am looking sternly at you, and I am giving you ten times as much cause of offence as that poor soldier—yet you do not strike *me*."

A naturally irritable disposition can always be tamed down, by a strong and persevering effort to subdue it, and by determining always to check it on its first approaches to passion. The indulgence of temper renders a man (and still more a woman) the dread and shame of the whole house. It wears out the affection of husbands, wives, and children—of brothers and sisters; destroys friendship; disturbs the enjoyment of social intercourse; causes incessant changing of servants; and is a constant source of misery to that most unhappy of all classes, poor relations.

That a violent temper is generally accompanied by a good heart, is a popular fallacy. On the contrary, the indulgence of it hardens the heart. And even if its ebullitions are always succeeded by "compunctious visitings," and followed by apologies and expressions of regret, still it leaves wounds that time cannot always efface, and which we may forgive, but cannot forget.

Ill-tempered women are very apt to call themselves nervous, and to attribute their violent fits of passion to a weakness of the nerves. This is not true. A real nervous affection shows itself "more in sorrow than in anger," producing tears, tremor, and head-ache, fears without adequate cause, and general depression of spirits—the feelings becoming tender to a fault.

When a woman abandons herself to terrible fits of anger with little or no cause, and makes herself a frightful spectacle, by turning white with rage, rolling up her eyes, drawing in her lips, gritting her teeth, clenching her hands, and stamping her feet, depend on it, she is not of a nervous, but of a furious temperament. A looking-glass held before her, to let her see what a shocking object she has made herself, would, we think, have an excellent effect. We have seen but a few females in this revolting state, and only three of them were ladies—but we have heard of many.

When the paroxysm is over, all the atonement she can make is to apologise humbly, and to pray contritely. If she has really any goodness of heart, and any true sense of religion, she will do this promptly, and prove her sincerity by being very kind to those whom she has outraged and insulted—and whose best course during these fits of fury is to make no answer, or to leave the room.

SPEAKING TO THE PERFECT WOMAN

There are ladies so exceedingly satisfied with themselves, and so desirous of being thought the special favourites of Providence, that they are always desiring to hold out an idea "that pain and sorrow can come not near them," and that they enjoy a happy exemption from "all the ills that flesh is heir to." They complain of nothing, for they profess to have nothing to complain of. They feel not the cold of winter, nor the heat of summer. The temperature is always exactly what *they* like. To them the street is never muddy with rain, nor slippery with ice. Unwholesome food agrees perfectly with *them*. They sleep soundly in bad beds, or rather no beds are bad. Travelling never fatigues them. Nobody imposes on them, nobody offends them. Other people may be ill—they are always in good health and spirits. To them all books are delightful—all pictures beautiful—all music charming. Other people may have trouble with their children—*they* have none. Other people may have bad servants—*theirs* are always excellent.

Now if all this were true, the lot of such persons would indeed be enviable, and we should endeavour to learn by what process such complete felicity has been attained—and why they see every thing through such a roseate medium. But it is not true. This is all overweening vanity, and a desire "to set themselves up above the rest of the world." We have always noticed that these over-fortunate, over-happy women have, in reality, a discontented, care-worn look, resulting from the incessant painful effort to seem what they are not. And if any body will take the trouble, it is very easy to catch them in discrepancies and contradictions. But it is not polite to do so. Therefore let them pass.

CHILD TALK

As mothers are always on the *qui vive*, (and very naturally,) be careful what you say of their children. Unless he is a decidedly handsome man, you may give offence by remarking, "The boy is the very image of his father." If the mother is a vain woman, she would much rather hear that all the children are the very image of herself. Refrain from praising too much the children of another family, particularly if the two sets of children are cousins. It is often dangerous to tell a mother that "little Willy is growing quite handsome." She will probably answer, "I had hoped my child was handsome always." With some mothers it is especially imprudent to remark that "little Mary looks like her aunt, or her grandmother." Again, if you prudently say nothing about the looks of the little dears, you may be suspected and perhaps accused of taking no interest in children. Young ladies, when in presence of gentlemen, are too apt to go on the other extreme, and over-act their parts, in the excessive fondling and kissing and hugging of children not in the least engaging, or even good-looking. We cannot believe that any female, not the mother, can really fall into raptures with a cross, ugly child. But how pleasant it is to play with and amuse, an intelligent, affectionate, and good-tempered little thing, to hear its innocent sayings, and to see the first buddings of its infant mind.

RESPECTING YOUR ELDERS

In talking to an elderly lady, it is justly considered very rude to make any allusion to her age; even if she is unmistakeably an old woman, and acknowledges it herself. For instance, do not say—"This silk of yours is very suitable for an elderly person"—or—"Will you take this chair?—an old lady like you will find it very comfortable"—or—"Look, baby—is not that grandma?"—or—"I told the servant to attend first to you, on account of your age"—or—"Children, don't make such a noise—have you no respect for old people?"

All this we have heard.

Chapter XIII

INCORRECT WORDS

TWO WRONGS DON'T MAKE A RIGHT

Every one who sees much of the world must observe with pain and surprise various unaccountable instances of improper and incorrect words that sometimes disfigure the phraseology of females who have gone through a course of fashionable education, and mixed in what is really genteel society. These instances, it is true, are becoming every day more rare; but we regret that they should exist at all. Such women will say "that there," and "this here"—"them girls"—"them boys"—"I don't want no more"—"I didn't hear nothing about it"—"I didn't see nobody there"—"I won't do so no more." And other similar violations of grammar; and grammar is never more palpably outraged than when two negatives are used for an affirmative. It is surely shorter and easier to say, "I want no more"—"I heard nothing about it"—"I saw nobody there"—"I will do so no more."

Another grammatical error, less glaring, but equally incorrect, is the too common practice of converting a certainty into an uncertainty by saying, "I have no doubt but he was there." As if his being there was your only doubt. You should say, "I have no doubt of his being there." "I have no doubt but that he wrote it," seems to signify that you do doubt his writing it, and that you are nearly sure he did not. The proper phrase is, "I have no doubt of his writing it." "I do not doubt but that she knew it long ago," implies that you do doubt her having known it. It should be, "I do not doubt her knowing it long ago." Leave out *but*, when you talk of doubting.

REGIONAL HABITS

We hope it is not necessary to caution our readers against the most provincial of provincialisms, such as, "I hadn't ought," or "I shouldn't ought"—or "It warn't," instead of "It was not"—or the exclamations, "Do tell!" or "I want to know," ejaculated as a token of surprise the moment after you have told, and made known. The common English habit, or rather a habit of the common English, of using continually the words "you know," and "you know," is very tiresome, particularly when they are talking of something that you cannot possibly be acquainted with. Check them by saying, "No, I do not know." They also make great use of the word "monstrous"—ugly as that word is. Do not imitate them in saying that you are "monstrous glad," or "monstrous sorry," or "monstrous tired," or that a young lady is "monstrous pretty." We have heard even "monstrous little."

WORD CONFUSION

"Emptyings" is not a good name for yeast. "Up chamber, up garret, down cellar," are all wrong. Why not say, "up in the chamber, up in the garret, down in the kitchen, down in the cellar" &c.? Why should a mirthful fit of laughter be called "a gale"? "Last evening we were all in such a gale!"

Snow and ice are not the same. Therefore a snowball should not be called an ice-ball, which latter might be a very dangerous missile.

Pincushions are pincushions, and not pin-balls, unless they are of a globular shape. If in the form of hearts, diamonds, &c., they are not balls.

When you are greatly fatigued, say so—and not that you are "almost beat out."

It is wrong to say that certain articles of food are healthy or unhealthy. Wholesome and unwholesome are the right words. A pig may be healthy or unhealthy while alive; but after he is killed and becomes pork, he can enjoy no health, and suffer no sickness.

If you have been accustomed to pronounce the word "does" as "doos," get rid of the custom as soon as you can. Also, give up saying "pint" for "point," "jint" for "joint," "anint" for "anoint," &c. Above all, cease saying "featur, creatur, natur, and raptur."

The word "slump," or "slumped," has too coarse a sound to be used by a lady.

When you have exchanged one article for another, say so, and not that you have "traded it."

Do not say, "I should admire to read that book," "I should admire to hear that song," "I should admire to see the president." Substitute, "I should like to read that book," "I should like to hear that song," "I should like to see the president."

Using the word "love" instead of "like" is not peculiar to the ladies of any section of the Union. But they may assure themselves it is wrong to talk of *loving* any thing that is eatable. They may *like* terrapins, oysters, chicken-salad, or ice-cream; but they need not *love* terrapins or oysters, or *love* chicken-salad.

POSITIVE VULGARISMS

The word "mayhap" (instead of perhaps) is a positive vulgarism. It is of English origin, but is only used in England by very low people—and by English writers, never.

We have little tolerance for young ladies, who, having in reality neither wit nor humour, set up for both, and having nothing of the right stock to go upon, substitute coarseness and impertinence, (not to say impudence,) and try to excite laughter, and attract the attention of gentlemen, by talking slang. Where do they get it? How do they pick it up? From low newspapers, or from vulgar books? Surely not from low companions?

We have heard one of these ladies, when her collar chanced to be pinned awry, say that it was put on drunk— also that her bonnet was drunk, meaning crooked on her head. When disconcerted, she was "floored." When submitting to do a thing unwillingly, "she was brought to the scratch." Sometimes "she did things on the sly." She talked of a certain great vocalist "singing like a beast." She believed it very smart and piquant to use these vile expressions. It is true, when at parties, she always had half a dozen gentlemen about her; their curiosity being excited as to what she would say next. And yet she was a woman of many good qualities; and one who boasted of having always "lived in society."

WHAT'S IN A NAME?

We think that gentlemen lose a particle of their respect for young ladies who allow their names to be abbreviated into such cognomens as Kate, Madge, Bess, Nell, &c. Surely it is more lady-like to be called Catharine, Margaret, Eliza, or Ellen. We have heard the beautiful name Virginia degraded into Jinny; and Harriet called Hatty, or even Hadge.

A very silly practice has been introduced of writing Sally, Sallie—Fanny, Fannie—Mary, Marie—Abby, Abbie, &c. What would our grand-parents have thought of Pollie, Mollie, Peggie, Kittie, Nancie? Suppose young men were to adopt it, and sign themselves, Sammie, Billie, Dickie, Tommie, &c.!

By-the-bye, unless he is a relation, let no young lady address a gentleman by his Christian name. It is a familiarity which he will not like.

Chapter XIV

BORROWING

TO BORROW OR NOT TO BORROW

Any article you are likely to want on more than one occasion, it is better to buy than to borrow. If your own, you can have it always at hand: you will lay yourself under no obligation to a lender, and incur no responsibility as to its safety while in your possession. But when you *do* borrow, see that the article is speedily returned. And, under no consideration, take the liberty of lending it to any person whatever, before restoring it to the owner. Apologies and expressions of regret are no compensation, should it be out of your power to replace it if injured or lost.

REQUESTING PERMISSION

When you ask to borrow a thing, do not say, "Will you *loan* it to me?" The word "loan" is, by good talkers, and good writers, never used but as a substantive: notwithstanding that Johnson gives it as a verb also, but only on one obscure authority—and Johnson is not now regarded as infallible. To *lend*, not to *loan*, is the usual and proper expression. As a substantive it is generally employed in a commercial and political sense, or to denote a large sum borrowed for a public and important purpose. It is true you can say, "May I request the loan of your fan?" "Will you permit me to ask the loan of this book?" But it is much easier and smoother to say simply, "Will you lend me your fan for a few minutes?" "Will you be kind enough to lend me this book?"

THE PRACTICE OF BORROWING
HOUSEHOLD ITEMS

With regard to the practice of borrowing articles of household use, it is generally a custom "more honoured in the breach than the observance," particularly when living in a place where all such things can be easily obtained by sending to the shops. There are persons who, with ample means of providing themselves with all that is necessary for domestic service, are continually troubling their neighbours for the loan of a hammer, a screw-driver, a gimlet, a carpet-stretcher, a bed-stead screw, a fluting-iron, a preserving kettle, jelly-moulds, ice-cream freezers, &c. &c. If these or any other articles *must* be borrowed, let them be returned promptly, and in good order.

If, in consequence of the unexpected arrival of company, any thing for the table is borrowed of a neighbour, such as tea, coffee, butter, &c., see that it is punctually returned; equal in quantity, and in quality; or rather superior. Habitual borrowers are very apt to forget this piece of honesty, either neglecting to return the things at all, or meanly substituting inferior articles— or perhaps laying themselves under such an imputation without actually deserving it, should the lender be ill-natured or untruthful. There is a homely proverb, "To go a-borrowing is to go a-sorrowing."

Avoid borrowing change, or small sums. It is possible that you may really forget to repay them; but then it is also possible that you may be suspected of forgetting wilfully. So do not trust much to your memory. It is a true remark, that there are few instances of a borrower being so oblivious as to offer twice over the return of a small loan, forgetting that it had been paid already.

When a friend lends you a handkerchief, a collar, or any other washable article, see that it is nicely washed, and done up, before returning it to her,—and do so promptly. If an article of jewellery, carry it back to her yourself, and put it into her own hand, to preclude all risk of loss. She will not be so ungenerous as to tell any person that she has lent it to you; and will for a while afterward, refrain from wearing it herself, in any company where it may be recognised.

Should a visiter accidentally leave her handkerchief at your house, have it washed and ironed before restoring it to her.

On borrowing a book, immediately put a cover upon it—and let the cover be of clean, smooth, white or light-coloured paper. Make no remarks with pen or pencil on the margin of any book that does not belong to yourself. Whatever may be your own opinion of certain passages, you have no right to disturb other readers by obtruding upon them these opinions, unasked for. The pleasure of reading a book from a public library, is frequently marred by finding, as you proceed, that some impertinent fools have been before you, and scribbled their silly comments all through; or indulged in sneers and vituperations directed at the author.

Never, on any consideration, allow yourself to lend a borrowed book. If requested to do so, it should be a sufficient excuse to say that "it is not your own." But if still urged, persist in declining steadily; for it is a liberty you have no right to take with any article belonging to another. Even if the owner is your sister, you should lend nothing of hers without first obtaining her permission.

If, while in your possession, a borrowed book is irreparably injured, it is your duty to replace it by purchasing for the owner another copy. And, if that cannot be procured, all you can do is to buy a work of equal value, and to present *that*, as the only compensation in your power. Observe the same rule with all borrowed articles, lost or injured.

Some young ladies have a bad habit of biting their fingers, especially if they rejoice in handsome hands; and the same ladies, by way of variety, are prone to bite the corners of books, and the edges of closed fans. So it is dangerous to trust these articles in their vicinity.

Chapter XV

OFFENCES

LET THE LOVE NEVER DIE

If the visits of an acquaintance become less frequent than formerly, the falling off is not always to be imputed to want of regard for you, or to having lost all pleasure in your society. The cause may be want of time, removal to a distance, precarious health, care of children, absence from town, family troubles, depressed fortunes, and various other circumstances. Also, with none of these causes, visiting may gradually and almost insensibly decline, and neither of the parties have the slightest dislike to each other. If no offence has been intended, none should be taken; and when you chance to meet, instead of consuming the time in complaints of estrangement, meet as if your intercourse had never been interrupted, and you will find it very easy to renew it; and perhaps on a better footing than before. The renewal should be marked by a prompt interchange of special invitations— followed by visits.

If no answer is returned to a note of invitation, be not hasty in supposing that the omission has sprung from rudeness or neglect. Trust that your friend is neither rude nor neglectful; and believe that the answer was duly sent, but that it miscarried from some accidental circumstance.

STRAIGHT-TALKING

A friend may inadvertently say something that you do not like to hear, or may make a remark that is not pleasant to you. Unless it is prefaced with a *previous* apology; or unless she desires you "not to be offended at what she is going to say;" or unless she informs you that "she considers it her duty always to speak her mind,"—you have no right to suppose the offence premeditated, and therefore you should restrain your temper, and calmly endeavour to convince her that she is wrong; or else acknowledge that she is right. She ought then to apologise for what she said, and you should immediately change the subject, and never again refer to it. In this way quarrels may be prevented, and ill-feeling crushed in the bud. When what is called "a coolness" takes place between friends, the longer it goes on the more difficult it is to get over. But "better late than never." If, on consideration, you find that *you* were in the wrong, let no false pride, no stubborn perverseness prevent you from making that acknowledgement. If your friend, on her part, first shows a desire for reconciliation, meet her half-way. A vindictive disposition is a bad one, and revenge is a most unchristian feeling. People of sense (unless the injury is very great, and of lasting consequences) are easy to appease, because they generally have good feelings, and know how to listen to reason.

MEETING WITH THE ENEMY

Should you chance to be thrown into the presence of persons who have proved themselves your enemies, and with whom you can have no intercourse, say nothing either *to* them or *at* them; and do not place yourself in their vicinity. To talk *at* a person, is mean and vulgar. Those who do it are fully capable of writing anonymous and insulting letters; and they often do so.

If you have, unfortunately, had a quarrel with a friend, talk of it to others as little as possible; lest in the heat of anger, you may give an exaggerated account, and represent your adversary in darker colours than she deserves. You may be very sure these misrepresentations will reach her ear, and be greatly magnified by every successive relater. In this way a trifle may be swelled into importance; a mole-hill may become a mountain; and a slight affront may embitter the feelings of future years. "Blessed are the peacemakers,"—and a mutual friend, if well-disposed toward both opponents, generally has it in her power to effect a reconciliation, by repeating, kindly, any favourable remark she may chance to have heard one of the offended parties make on the other. In truth, we wish it were the universal custom for all people to tell other people whatever good they may hear of them—instead of the wicked and hateful practice of telling only the bad. Make it a rule to repeat to your friends all the pleasant remarks that (as far as you know) are made on them, and you will increase their happiness, and your own popularity. We do not mean that you should flatter them, by reciting compliments that are not true; but truth is not flattery, and there is no reason why agreeable truths should not always be told. There would then be far more kind feeling in the world.

OVERHEARING CRITICISMS

Should you chance accidentally to overhear a remark to your disadvantage, consider first if there may not be some truth in it. If you feel that there is, turn it to profitable account, and try to improve, or to get rid of the fault, whatever it may be. But never show resentment at any thing not intended for your ear, unless it is something of such vital importance as to render it necessary that you should come forward in self-defence. These instances, however, are of rare occurrence.

If you are so placed that you can hear the conversation of persons who are talking about you, it is very mean to sit there and listen. Immediately remove to a distance far enough to be out of hearing.

It is a proverb that listeners seldom hear any good of themselves. It were a pity if they should. Eavesdropping or listening beneath an open window, the crack of a door, or through a key-hole, are as dishonourable as to pick pockets.

Chapter XVI

CHILDREN

DRESSING YOUR CHILD

Infants, when they are not really sick, frequently cry from some incidental annoyance, and not from a fretful disposition. If they feel comfortably they will usually be good-humoured and pleasant. Much of their comfort is sacrificed to the vanity of the mother in dressing them fashionably and expensively. We knew a baby that was very good in the morning, but very cross in the afternoon, or when dressed for show. And no wonder, for in her show-costume she was tortured with necklace, sleeve-loops, and bracelets of fine branchy, or rather briary coral, scratching and irritating her delicate skin, and leaving the print in red marks. On our representing this to the mother as the probable cause of the baby's fretfulness, the thorny ornaments were left off, and the child became amiable. Gold chains are also very irritating to the neck and arms of an infant. Coral beads of a smooth round form, strung evenly on a simple thread of silk, without any intermingling of gold chain, are, perhaps, the most comfortable necklaces for children, and are also very becoming; but as they are not expensive, they are of course not fashionable.

We wish also that mothers, generally, were less proud of seeing their babies with "luxuriant heads of hair," which if it has no natural tendency to curl, disfigures the child and gives it a wild, ungenteel look. If it does curl, it still heats the head and neck, and is said to draw away much strength from the system. The most healthy infants we have seen, had very little hair, or it was judiciously kept closely cut. To curl children's hair in papers is barbarous. They pay dearly for the glory of appearing in ringlets during the day, if they are made to pass their nights lying upon a mass of hard, rough bobs, about as pleasant as if they had their heads in a bag of hickory-nuts. But then the mother has the gratification of hearing their curls admired!

Among other sufferings inflicted on babies is that of sending them out in bleak winter days with brimless hats, that, so far from screening their faces from the cold wind, do not even afford the slightest shade to their eyes, which are winking and watering all the time from the glare of the sun and snow. We have seen false curls pinned to these babies' hats, and dangling in their eyes.

Another detestable practice is that of making the waists of children's frocks ridiculously long and painfully tight; particularly over the chest and body, which are thus pressed flat, to the utter ruin of the figure, and the risk of producing incurable diseases—such as consumption of the lungs, and projection of the spine; to say nothing of the various complaints connected with the stomach, which is thus squeezed into half its natural compass. Also, the sleeve-holes are so small and tight as to push up the shoulders. Then the hips are pressed downward far below their proper place, and the legs are consequently in danger of becoming short and bandy. Is it possible this vile fashion can continue much longer?—and are "the rising generation" really to grow up with high shoulders, round backs, flat chests, bodies that seem longer than their legs, and hips almost where their knees ought to be?

Also, these limbs must suffer from cold in winter with no other covering than cotton stockings, the skirts of the dress scarcely reaching to the knees—the little boys disfigured with the ugliest of all garments, short knee-breeches.

Add to all the rest of these abominations, tight boots with peaked toes, and can we wonder that children, even beyond the period of infancy, should, at times, be cross, irritable, and unamiable. How can they be otherwise, when they seldom feel comfortably? Then, if the parents can afford it, (or whether or not,) the unhappy children are bedizened with all manner of expensive finery, and interdicted from romping, lest they should injure it. But, what matter if the children suffer—the mother's vanity *must* be gratified, and she *must* have the delight of seeing that her boys and girls are as fashionably dressed as the little Thomsons and Wilsons and Jacksons.

CHILDREN'S PLAYTIME AND PARTIES

Formerly, children learned to play various amusing games, such as "Hot buttered beans," "Blind-man's bluff," &c. Now their play is chiefly running and squealing, and chasing each other about, without any definite object, except that of making a noise. Then, at a juvenile party, the amusement was chiefly in the varieties of these entertaining games. Now it is dancing—for as many as can find places to dance—and nothing at all for those who cannot, but to grow tired and sleepy. In former times, children's parties commenced at two o'clock in the afternoon in winter, and at four in summer. They played till they were summoned to a large and well-supplied tea-table, and were sent for to come home by eight o'clock, being then quite tired enough to go to bed and sleep soundly, and waken with pleasant recollections of yesterday. If the party was very large, the elder children sat round the room, and tea, &c. was handed to them, while the little ones were accommodated at a table where the hostess presided. The children of that time really enjoyed these parties, and so would those of the present time, if they could have such. The juvenile-party dress was then but a simple white muslin frock with a ribbon sash. We have since seen little girls at a summer party steadfastly refuse strawberries and cream, in obedience to the interdiction of their mothers; who had enjoined them to do so, lest they should stain or otherwise injure their elegant silk dresses.

It is not well to put a small child "through its facings," by trying to make it exhibit any of its little feats before strangers. They are generally very reluctant to make this exhibition. Sometimes they are bashful, sometimes perverse; but if the mother persists in her attempt to show them off, it will probably prove a complete failure, and end in a cry, or that outbreak usually called a tantrum. By-the-bye, there is no better way of stopping a tantrum than quietly to divert the child's attention to something else.

MANNERS MAKETH MAN

Children should not be brought to table till they are able to feed themselves, first with a spoon, and next with a fork. And not then, unless they can be depended on to keep quiet, and not talk. The chattering of children all dinner-time is a great annoyance to grown people. The shrill voice of a child can be distinguished annoyingly amid those of a whole company. They should be made to understand that if they talk at table, they are to be immediately taken away to finish their dinner in the nursery. On no consideration should they be admitted to table when there is a dinner-party. The foolish custom of having all the children dressed for the purpose, and brought in with the dessert, is now obsolete.

We have seen children so well and so early trained that they could be trusted to come to table every day without the least fear of their misbehaving by talking or otherwise. They sat quietly, asked for nothing, took contentedly whatever was put on their plates, made no attempt at helping themselves, and neither greased nor slopped the table-cloth; and when done, wiped their mouths and hands on their napkins, before they quitted their chairs, which they did at a sign from their mother; going out without noise, and neither leaving the door open nor slamming it hard. It is very easy to accustom children to these observances. Also, they may be taught very early, how to behave to visiters. For instance, not to pass between them and the fire, not to hang on the back of a lady's chair; or to squeeze close to her; or to get on her lap; or to finger her dress; or to search her reticule, or her pocket; or to ask a stranger for pennies or sixpences; or to tell her that she is not pretty; or to enquire "why she wears such an ugly bonnet?"

There are very little girls who, if their mother is from home, can do the honours in her place; seat the visiter on the sofa, and press her to stay till their mother comes in; and if the lady declines doing so, they will ask her at least to stay awhile, and rest herself, and have a glass of cool water; and while she stays, they will do their best to entertain her. Such children always grow up with polished manners, if not removed from the influence that made them so in early life.

Children should be early taught not to repeat the conversation of grown persons, and never to tell the servants any thing they have heard in the parlour. When they come home from school, they ought not to be encouraged in telling school-tales. If they dine out, never question them concerning what they had for dinner. Forbid their relating any circumstances concerning the domestic economy of the house at which they have been entertained.

A TIP FROM THE AUTHOR

If a child purloins cakes or sweetmeats, punish him by giving him none the next time they are on table.

A B C, 1 2 3

At four years of age, a beginning should be made in teaching them to read, by hearing them the alphabet every day till they have learned it perfectly; and afterwards the first spelling-tables. With a quarter of  an hour's daily instruction, a child of common capacity will, in six months, be able to spell in two or three syllables, and to read short easy stories with the syllables divided. At the end of the year, if her lessons are regular, and not so long as to tire her, she will, in all probability, take pleasure in reading to herself, when her lessons are over. Were they taught *out of story-books only*, there are few children that at the age of six years would find any difficulty in reading fluently. If *very* intelligent, they often can read well at five. When they can once read, encourage them in the love of books; but do not set them at any other branch of education till they are eight. Then, their hands being strong enough to guide the pen firmly, they may commence writing copies. They should be supplied with slates and pencils at three years old. If they have any dormant talent for drawing, this will call it out. Little girls may begin to sew at four or five, but only as an amusement, not as a task. The best and most satisfactory dolls for young children are those of linen or rag, made very substantially. Much money is wasted in toys that afford them no amusement whatever; and toys that, being merely to look at, they grow tired of immediately, and delight in breaking to pieces.

SEEN AND NOT HEARD

There is no place in which children appear to greater disadvantage or are less ungovernable than at hotels or boarding-houses. We are always sorry when the circumstances of parents oblige them permanently to live thus in public, with their young families, who are consequently brought up in a manner which cannot but have an unfavourable effect in forming the characters of the future men and women. By way of variety, and that they may not always be confined up-stairs, the children are encouraged, or at least permitted by their mothers, to spend much of their time in the drawing-room, regardless of the annoyance which their noise and romping never fails to inflict upon the legitimate occupants of that apartment. The parents, loving their children too much to be incommoded themselves by any thing that their offspring can say or do, seem not aware that they can possibly interrupt or trouble the rest of the company. Or else, conscious of their own inability to control them, they are afraid to check the children lest they should turn restive, rebel, or break out into a tantrum. "Any thing for the sake of peace," is a very foolish maxim where juveniles are concerned. By being firm once or twice, and dismissing them from the room when they deserve it, you may have peace ever after. The noisiest and most inconvenient time to have children in a public parlour is in the interval between their tea and their bed-time. Some children have no bed-time. And when they are tired of scampering and shouting, they lie about sleeping on the sofas, and cry if they are finally wakened, to go up with their mother when she retires for the night.

Still worse is the practice that prevails in some hotels and boarding-houses, of the mothers sending the nurse-maids with the babies, to sit in the drawing-room among the ladies; who are thus liable to have a vulgar and obtrusive servant-girl, most probably "from the old country," boldly taking her seat in the midst of them, or conspicuously occupying one of the front-windows; either keeping up a perpetual undercurrent of fulsome, foolish talk to the baby, or listening eagerly to the conversation around her, and, perhaps, repeating it invidiously as soon as she gets an opportunity. If one lady sends her nurse-maid to sit in the drawing-room with the child, all the other mothers of babies immediately follow suit, and the drawing-room becomes a mere nursery.

Every hotel should have a commodious and airy parlour set apart entirely for the children and nurses. The proprietors could easily afford to keep one good room for that purpose, if they would expend a little less on the finery of the parlours, &c. We have heard of an embroidered piano-cover, in a great hotel, costing fourteen hundred dollars, and the children pulling it down and dragging it about the floor. With a piano-cover of the usual cost, and other things less ostentatious, a children's parlour might well have been afforded in this very establishment.

At a hotel, if the children come to the ladies' table, they are always in danger of eating food that is highly improper for them, and they very soon learn to help themselves to much more than they want, and to eat voraciously, in their desire to "have something of every thing." There is always a table purposely for those children whose parents pay half-price for them; and at which the housekeeper presides. However good this table may be, and though the pies and puddings may be excellent, the mothers are frequently dissatisfied with the absence of ice-cream, blanc-mange, charlotte-russe, &c., though certainly, were they in houses of their own, they would not have such things every day. Therefore, though it is "not in the bond," the mothers carry away from the table saucers of these delicacies, and the children learn to expect a daily supply of them from the ladies' dining-room. This, we must say, is a mean practice. We have, however, known some mothers, who, really being "honourable women," sent every day to a confectioner's to *buy* ice-cream for their children.

There is danger at a hotel of little boys loitering about the bar or office, encouraged by unthinking young men, who give them "tastes of drink," and even amuse themselves by teaching them to smoke segars.

Chapter XVII

EVENING PARTIES

THE INVITATIONS

Having made out a list of the persons you intend to invite, proceed to write the notes; or have them written in a neat, handsome hand, by an experienced calligrapher. Fashion, in its various changes, sometimes decrees that these notes, and their envelopes, shall be perfectly plain, (though always of the finest paper,) and that the wax seals shall of course be very small. At other times, the mode is to write on embossed note paper, with bordered envelopes, secured by fancy wafers, transparent, medallion, gold or silver. If the seals are gold or silver, the edges or borders of the paper should be also gilt or silvered. Sometimes, for a very large or splendid party, the notes are engraved and printed on cards. Consult the Directory, to obtain the *exact* address of those to whom you send them.

These invitations may be transmitted by one of the City post offices; first putting a stamp on each. Let the stamps be such as will leave nothing additional to be paid by the receiver. Another way is to send round the notes by a reliable servant-man of your own; or to engage, for this purpose, one of the public waiters that are hired to attend at parties. The notes are usually sent either eight, seven, or six days before the party—if it is to be very large, ten days or two weeks. In the notes, always specify not only the day of the week, but also the day of the month, when the party is to take place. It is very customary now to designate the hour of assembling, and then the company are expected to be punctual to that time. People, *really genteel*, do not go ridiculously late. When a ball is intended, let the word "Dancing" be introduced in small letters, at the lower left-hand corner of the note.

For a bridal party, subsequent to a wedding, the words now used are thus—

Mr. and Mrs. S. M. Morland, At Home, on Thursday evening, Sept. 22, 1853.

Their residence must be given beneath, in a corner, and in smaller letters.

Oblong slices of plumb-cake, iced all over, are now sent round in very pretty white card-board boxes, exactly fitting each slice, covered on the inside with lace-paper, and an engraved card of the bride and groom laid on the top of the cake. These boxes (to be had at the fancy stationers,) are of various prices; some of them are very elegant and costly.

WEDDINGS

At wedding-parties, it is usual for the bride and bridesmaids to appear in exactly the same dresses they wore at the marriage; all of them ranged in their respective stations before the company begin to arrive.

When the marriage-guests are not too numerous, it is customary to have all the company shown into the largest parlour, when they first arrive; the folding-doors being closed between. Meanwhile, the bride and groom, bridesmaids and groomsmen, with the heads of the family, arrange themselves in a line or a semi-circle; the most important personages in the centre, with the clergyman in front of them. When all is ready, the doors are thrown open, the guests advance, and the ceremony begins. When it is over, and the bride is receiving the compliments of her friends, we hope the silliest woman present will not go up and ask her the foolish question, "If she does not feel already like an old married woman?"

A crowd at a wedding is now obsolete. We once heard of a marriage in a great family, where the company was so numerous that all the doors were blocked up, and quite inaccessible; and the bride could only make her entrance by being taken round outside, and lifted through a back window—the groom jumping in after her.

Dancing at weddings is old-fashioned. A band of music playing in the hall is of no use, as on such occasions no one listens to it, and some complain of the noise. We think a marriage in church is not as fine a spectacle as may be imagined. The effect is lost in the size of the building, and broken up by the intervention of the aisles and pews; the wedding guests seated in the latter, and the former occupied by people out of the street, coming in to see the show. And this they will do, if not forcibly excluded; particularly idle boys, and nurse-maids with children, all trying to get as near the altar as possible.

If the bride and groom are to set out on a journey immediately after the ceremony, it is best for her to be married in a handsome travelling-dress—new for the occasion, of course. This is often done now. She can reserve the usual wedding costume for her first party after returning home.

PREPARATIONS FOR ALL TYPES OF PARTY

In preparing for a party, it is well (especially if you have had but little experience yourself,) to send for one of the *best* public waiters, and consult with him on the newest style of "doing these things." He can also give you an idea of the probable expense. We do not, of course, allude to magnificent entertainments, such as are celebrated in the newspapers, and become a nine days' wonder; and are cited as costing, not hundreds, but thousands of dollars.

In case the required waiter should be pre-engaged, it is well to send for, and consult him, a week or two before your party.

In engaging your presiding genius, it is well to desire him to come on the morning of the party; he will be found of great advantage in assisting with the final preparations. He will attend to the silver, and china, and glass; and see that the lamps are all in order, and that the fires, coal-grates, furnaces, &c., are in proper trim for evening. He will bring with him his apprentices that he has in training for the profession.

One of these men should be stationed in the vestibule, or just within the front door. On that evening, (if not at other times,) let this door be furnished with a lamp, placed on a shelf or bracket in the fan-light, to illumine the steps, and shine down upon the pavement, where the ladies cross it on alighting from the carriages. If the evening proves rainy, let another man attend with an umbrella, to assist in sheltering them on their way into the house. The ladies should all wear over-shoes, to guard their thin slippers from the damp, in their transit from the coach to the vestibule.

At the top, or on the landing-place, of the first stair-case, let another man be posted, to show the female guests to their dressing-room; while still another waiter stays near the gentlemen's room till the company have done arriving.

In the apartment prepared as a fixing-room for the ladies two or more women should be all the evening in attendance; both rooms being well warmed, well lighted, and furnished with all that may be requisite for giving the last touches to head, feet, and figure, previous to entering the drawing-room. When ready to go down, the ladies meet their gentlemen in the passage between the respective dressing-rooms; the beaux being there already, waiting for the belles, who must not detain them long—men being very impatient on these, and all other occasions.

If any lady is without an escort, and has no acquaintances at hand to take her under their wing, she should send for the master of the house to meet her near the door, and give her his arm into the drawing-room. He will then lead her to the hostess, and to a seat. Let her then bow, as a sign that she releases him from farther attendance, and leaves him at liberty to divide his civilities among his other guests.

In the ladies' room, (beside two toilet glasses with their branches lighted,) let a Psyche or Cheval glass be also there. Likewise, a hand-mirror on each toilet to enable the ladies to see the back of their heads; with an ample supply of pins, combs, brushes, hair pins, &c.; and a work-box containing needles, thread, thimble, and scissors, to repair accidents to articles of dress. Let there be bottles of fine eau de cologne, and camphor and hartshorn, in case of faintings. Among the furniture, have a sofa and several foot-stools, for the ladies to sit on if they wish to change their shoes.

The women attending must take charge of the hoods, cloaks, shawls, over-shoes, &c.; rolling up together the things that belong to each lady, and putting each bundle in some place they can easily remember when wanted at the breaking up of the assembly.

It is now the custom for the lady of the house (and those of her own family,) to be dressed rather plainly, showing no desire to eclipse any of her guests, on this her own night. But her attire, though simple, should be handsome, becoming, and in good taste. Her business is, without any bustle or apparent officiousness, quietly and almost imperceptibly to try and render the evening as pleasant as possible to all her guests; introducing those who, though not yet acquainted, ought to be; and finding seats for ladies who are not young enough to continue standing.

SPACE FOR ONE MORE?

The custom that formerly prevailed in the absurd days of crowds and jams, when dense masses were squeezed into small apartments, of removing every seat and every piece of furniture from the room, is now obsolete. A hard squeeze is no longer a high boast. Genteel people no longer go to parties on the stair-case, or in the passages. The ladies are not now so compressed that nothing of them is seen but their heads; the sleeves, skirts, &c., undergoing a continual demolition down below. We knew of a lady, who, at a late hour, went to a crowded party in a real blonde dress, which was rubbed entirely off her before she reached the centre of the room, and it was hanging about her satin skirt in shreds, like transparent rags dissolving into "air—thin air!" For this blonde she had given two hundred dollars; and she was obliged to go home and exchange its tatters for a costume that was likely to last out the evening.

In houses where space is not abundant, it is now customary to have several *moderate* parties in the course of the season, instead of inviting all your "dear five hundred friends" on the self-same night.

REFRESHMENTS

When the hour of assembling is designated in the notes of invitation, (as it always should be,) the guests, of course, will take care to arrive as nearly as possible about that hour. At large parties, tea is usually omitted—it being supposed that every one has already taken that beverage at home, previous to commencing the business of the toilette. Many truly hospitable ladies still continue the custom, thinking that it makes a pleasant beginning to the evening, and exhilarates the ladies after the fatigue of dressing and arriving. So it does. For a large company, a table with tea, coffee, and cakes, may be set in the ladies-room, women being in attendance to supply the guests with those refreshments before they go down. Pitchers of ice-water and glasses should also be kept in this room.

If there is no tea, the refreshments begin with lemonade, macaroons, kisses, &c., sent round soon after the majority of the company has come. If there *is* tea, ice-water should be presented after it, to all; otherwise, there will be much inconvenience by numerous ladies dispatching the servants, separately, to bring them some.

MUSICAL MANNERS

After a little time allotted to conversation, music is generally introduced by one of the ladies of the family, if she plays well; otherwise, she invites a competent friend to commence. A lady who can do nothing "without her notes," or who cannot read music, and play at sight, is scarcely enough of a musician to perform in a large company—for this incapacity is an evidence that she has not a good ear, or rather a good memory for melody—or that her musical talent wants more cultivation. A large party is no time or place for practising, or for risking *attempts* at new things, or for vainly trying to remember old ones.

Some young ladies rarely sit down to a piano in any house but their own, without complaining that the instrument is out of tune. "It is a way they have." We have known a fair amateur to whom this complaint was habitual, and never omitted; even when we knew that, to provide against it, the piano had really been tuned that very day.

The tuning of a harp immediately before playing is sometimes a very tedious business. Would it not be well for the harpist to come a little earlier than the rest, and tune it herself previous to their arrival? And let her deem *that* tuning sufficient for a while, and not repeat the operation more than once again in the course of the evening, especially in the midst of her first piece. However delicate may be her own ear, or exquisitely fastidious her own taste, she may be assured that few of her audience would detect any deficiency, if she only went quietly on, and did not herself imply that deficiency.

Unless a gentleman is himself familiar with the air, let him not, on "mounting guard beside the piano," volunteer to turn over the pages for the lady who is playing. He will certainly turn them over too soon or too late, and therefore annoy and confuse her. Still worse, let him not attempt to accompany her with his voice, unless he is an excellent musician, or accustomed to singing with her.

For the hearers to crowd closely round the instrument, is smothering to the vocalist. Let them keep at a proper distance, and she will sing the better, and they will hear the better. It is so rude to talk during a song, that it is never done in company; but a little low conversation is sometimes tolerated in the adjoining room, during the performance of one of those interminable pieces of instrumental music, whose chief merit lies in its difficulty, and which (at least to the ears of the uninitiated,) is rather a bore than a pleasure. We have read a French novel, in which the only child of a farmer has just come home from a provincial boarding-school, and the seigneur, or lord of the manor, has volunteered a visit to these his respected tenants. The mother, amidst all the bustle of preparing a great dinner for the occasion, comes in to remind Annette that if the seigneur should ask her to play for him, she is to curtsey very low, and thank him for the honour. "And then, Annette," adds the good old dame, "be sure to play that tune which your father and I hate so much!"

By-the-bye, it is very old fashioned to return thanks to a lady for her singing, or to tell her she is very kind to oblige the company so often. If she is conscious of really singing well, and sees that she delights her hearers, she will not feel sensible of fatigue—at least till the agreeable excitement of conscious success is over.

It is ill-mannered, when a lady has just finished a song, for another lady to exclaim in her hearing—"Mary Jones sings that delightfully!"—or—"How charmingly Susan Smith gives us that ballad!" Let the glories of Mary Jones and Susan Smith rest, for that evening, within the limits of their own circle.

Do not ask any lady for a song that has already been sung on this very evening by another person.

People who have no idea of music sometimes make strange blunders in their requests. We know of a female who, at a large party, hearing a young lady accompany her voice on the national instrument of Spain, became very urgent to have *The Battle of Prague* performed on the guitar.

TO DANCE OR NOT TO DANCE

At a dancing party, the ladies of the house decline joining in it, out of politeness to their guests, till towards the latter part of the evening, when the company begins to thin off, and the dancers are fatigued.

We admire a charming girl, who, in her own house, being asked to dance by an agreeable man, has the self-denial to say to him—"Being at home, and desirous that my friends shall share as much as possible in the enjoyments of the evening, I would rather refrain from dancing myself. Let me present you to Miss Lindley, or to Miss Darwood; you will find either of these young ladies a delightful partner."

These amiable refusals we have heard from our amiable and unselfish young friends, and such, we hope, are heard often in what is *truly* "the best society."

Ladies who are strangers in the place, are, by courtesy, entitled to particular attention from those who know them.

We have sometimes seen, at a private ball, the least attractive woman dancing every set, (though acquitting herself very ill,) while handsome and agreeable ladies were sitting still. The mystery was solved on finding that the lady of the house carried her ultra benevolence so very far, as to make a business of procuring partners all the time for this unlovely and unprepossessing female, lest she should feel neglected. Now a certain portion of this officiousness is highly praiseworthy, but too much of it is a great annoyance to the victimised gentlemen— especially to those who, as a backwoodsman would say, are certainly "some pumpkins."

Even the most humane man, whatever may be the kindness of his heart, would rather not exhibit himself on the floor with a partner *ni jeune ni jolie*, who is ill-dressed, looks badly, moves ungracefully, can neither keep time to the music nor understand the figure, and in fact has "no dancing in her soul." If, with all the rest, she is dull and stupid, it is cruel for any kind friend to inflict her on a gentleman as a partner. Yet such things we have seen.

On one occasion we threw away a great deal of good pity on a youth, whom we thought had been inveigled into quadrilling with a lady who made the worst figure we ever saw in a ball-room. We afterwards learned that he had actually solicited the introduction; and we saw that he devoted himself to her all the remainder of the evening. She was a rich heiress.

Self-knowledge is a rare acquirement. But when a lady *does* suspect herself to be deficient in all the essential qualifications of a ball-room, she should give up dancing entirely, and be magnanimous enough always to excuse herself positively, when asked to dance; especially if verging on "a certain age." Let all "trippings on the light fantastic toe" be left to the young and gay.

CHILDREN'S BEDTIME

We deprecate the practice of keeping the small children of the family up all the evening, running and scampering in every one's way, or sleeping about on the chairs and sofas, and crying when wakened up to be carried to bed. Would it not be much better to have them sent to bed at their usual time? We knew two well-trained little boys, who submitted obediently to go to bed at their customary hour, on the night of their mother's party, of which they had seen nothing but the decorations of the parlours. They told their parents next morning, that still they had a great deal of pleasure, for after the carriages began to arrive, they had lain awake and "heard every ring."

A TIP FROM THE AUTHOR

At a ball, let no *coloured* chalks or crayons be used for the floor. They will rub off on the white shoes of the ladies, and spoil them.

A SUMMER AFFAIR

At a summer evening party, the refreshments are of a much lighter description than at a winter entertainment; consisting chiefly of ice-creams, water-ices, fresh fruit, lady-cake, and almond sponge-cake. Also strawberry or raspberry charlottes, which are made by arranging in glass bowls slices of cake cut in even and regular forms, and spread thickly over with the fruit mashed to a jam with white sugar—the bowls being heaped with whipt cream.

The dresses of the ladies are of clear muslin, or some other light material, and without any elaborate trimming. The hair is simply arranged—curls being inconvenient in warm weather; and the only head ornaments are ribbons, or *real* flowers.

At summer evening-parties the veranda is always put into requisition, being cooler than any part of the house.

At summer dinner-parties, let the dessert be served in another and cooler apartment; the company quitting the dining-room as soon as they have done with the meats, &c. The beauties of the dessert appear to greater advantage, when seen all at one view on a fresh table.

A GREAT BRITISH PARTY

We will introduce a minute account of a very fashionable English dinner-party, obtained from a friend who was one of the guests. It may afford some hints for the routine of an elegant entertainment, *à l'Anglais*.

The guests were twenty-four in number, and they began to assemble at half past seven, punctually. They were received in the library, where the host and hostess were standing ready to receive them, introducing those who were strangers to each other. When all had arrived, the butler entered, and going up to the lady of the house, told her in a low voice that "dinner was served." The hostess then arranged those that were not previously acquainted, and the gentlemen conducted the ladies to the dining-room; the principal stranger taking the mistress of the house, and the master giving his arm to the chief of the female guests. In England, these arrangements are made according to the rank of the ladies—that of the gentlemen is not considered. A duchess takes precedence of a marchioness, a viscountess of a countess, a baroness of a baron*et*'s lady, &c.,—for a baron is above a baronet. Going into the dining-room, the company passed by the butler and eight footmen, all of whom were stationed in two rows. The butler was dressed entirely in black—the footmen in their livery. According to a new fashion, they may now wear long gaiters. White kid gloves are indispensable to the footmen.

The table was set for twenty-six—and standing on it were elegant gilt candelabras. *All* the lights were wax candles. Chandeliers were suspended from the ceiling. In the middle of the table was a magnificent plateau, or centre ornament of gold; flowers surmounted the summit; and the circular stages below were covered with confectionery elegantly arranged. On each side of the plateau, and above and below, were tall china fruit-baskets. In the centre of each basket were immense pine-apples of hot-house growth, with their fresh green leaves. Below the pine-apples were large bunches of purple and white hot-house grapes, beautifully disposed, with leaves and tendrils hanging over the sides of the baskets. Down each side of the whole long table, were placed large, round, saucer-shaped fruit-dishes, heaped up with peaches, nectarines, pears, plumbs, ripe gooseberries, cherries, currants, strawberries, &c. All the fruits not in season were supplied from hot-houses. And alternating with the fruit were all the *entremets* in covered dishes, placed on long slips of damask the whole length of the table. All the plate was superb. The dinner-set was of French china, gilt, and painted with roses. At every plate was a caraffe of water, with a tumbler turned down over it, and several wine-glasses. The napkins were large. The side-board held only the show-silver and the wine. The side-tables were covered with elegant damask cloths. On these were ranged, laid along in numerous rows, the knives, forks, and spoons to be used at dinner. The dessert-spoons were in the form of hollow leaves, the stems being the handles. They were beautifully engraved in tasteful patterns. The fruit-knives had silver blades and pearl handles. There were two soups (white and brown,) standing on a side-table. Each servant handed the things in his white kid gloves, and with a damask napkin under his thumb. They offered (mentioning its name in a low voice,) a plate of each soup to each guest. After the soup, Hock and Moselle wine were offered to each guest, that they might choose either. A dish of fish was then placed at each end of the table—one was salmon, the other turbot. These dishes were immediately taken off to be helped by the servants, both sorts of fish being offered to each person. Then the appropriate sauce for the fish—also cucumbers to eat with the salmon. No castors were on the large table, but they were handed round by the servants. Directly after the fish came the *entremets*, or French dishes. The wine following the fish was Madeira and Sherry.

Afterwards, a saddle or haunch of Welsh mutton was placed at the master's end of the table, and at the lady's end a boiled turkey. These dishes being removed to the side-tables, very thin slices of each were handed round. The poultry was not dissected—nothing being helped but the breast. Ham and tongue was then supplied to those who took poultry; and currant-jelly to the eaters of mutton. Next came the vegetables, handed round on dishes divided into four compartments, each division containing a different sort of vegetable.

Next, two dishes of game were put on—one before the master of the house, and the other before the mistress. The game (which was perfectly well-done,) was helped by them, and sent round with the appropriate sauce. Then, placed along the table, were the sweet things—charlottes, jellies, frozen fruit, &c. A lobster salad, dressed and cut up large, was put on with the sweets. On a side-table were stilton and cream cheese, to be eaten with the salad. After this, port wine—the champagne being early in the dinner. Next the sweets were handed round. With the sweets were frozen fruits—fruits cut up, and frozen with isinglass-jelly, (red, in moulds.)

Next, a dessert plate was given to each guest, and on it a ground glass plate, about the size of a saucer. Between these plates was a crochet-worked white doyly, of the size of the under-plate; the crochet-work done with thread, so as to resemble lace. These doylies were laid under the ground-glass plate, to deaden the noise of their collision. Then was brought from the side-table a ground-glass plate of ice-cream, or water-ice, which you took in exchange for that before you. The water-ice was frozen in moulds, in the form of fruit, and suitably coloured. The baskets containing the fruit were then removed to the side-tables, where the servants had silver scissors, with which they clipped off small bunches of the grapes, and the green tops of the pine-apples, and a portion of the flesh of the fruit. The middle part was then pared and sliced. On each dessert-plate was placed a slice of pine-apple, and small bunches of white and blue grapes. After the grapes and pine-apples were thus handed round, the dishes of the other fruits were then offered successively to every guest. After the ground-glass and doylies, there was no farther change of plates.

After sitting a while over the fruit, the lady of the house gives the signal, by looking and bowing to the ladies on each side, and the ladies at this signal prepare to retire. The gentlemen all rise, and remain standing while the ladies depart—the master of the house holding the door open. The servants then all retire, except the butler, who remains to wait on the gentlemen, while they linger awhile (not more than a quarter of an hour,) over the fruit and wine.

Chapter XVIII

MISCELLANEOUS

COMMON IRRITATING HABITS

It may be well to caution our young friends against certain bad practices, easily contracted, but sometimes difficult to relinquish. The following are things not to be done:—Biting your nails. Slipping a ring up and down your finger. Sitting cross-kneed, and, jogging your feet. Drumming on the table with your knuckles; or, still worse, tinking on a piano with *your fore-finger only*. Humming a tune before strangers. Singing as you go up and down stairs. Putting your arm round the neck of another young girl, or promenading the room with arms encircling waists. Holding the hand of a friend all the time she sits beside you; or kissing and fondling her before company. Sitting too closely.

WAYS TO PUT OFF A GENTLEMAN

Slapping a gentleman with your handkerchief, or tapping him with your fan. Allowing him to take a ring off your finger, to look at it. Permitting him to unclasp your bracelet, or, still worse, to inspect your brooch. When these ornaments are to be shown to another person, always take them off for the purpose. Pulling at your own ringlets, or your own ear-rings—or fingering your neck ribbon. Suffering a gentleman to touch your curls. Reading with a gentleman off the same book or newspaper. Looking over the shoulder of any person who is reading or writing. Taking up a *written* paper from the table, and examining it.

PEEPING TOMS AND MAD WOMEN

To listen at door-cracks, and peep through key-holes, is vulgar and contemptible. So it is to ask children questions concerning their parents, though such things are still done.

If you mean that you were angry, do not say you were "mad."—"It made me so mad"—"I was quite mad at her," are phrases not to be used by people considering themselves genteel. Anger and madness are not the same, or should not be; though it is true that ungoverned rage, is, sometimes, carried so far as to seem like insanity.

A PROPER PARTY

Enter into no freaks of fashion that are silly, unmeaning, and unlady-like; even if they *have* been introduced by a belle, and followed by other belles. Commit no absurdity because a public singer or dancer has done so in her ignorance of good behaviour. During the Jenny Lind fever, there were young ladies who affected to skuttle into a drawing-room all of a sudden, somewhat as the fair Swede came skuttling in upon the concert stage, because in reality she knew not how to make her entrance gracefully. Other demoiselles twined and waved about, with body, head, and eyes, never a moment quiet. This squirming (as it was called) originated in a very bad imitation of Fanny Elssler's dancing motions. At one time there were girls at parties, who stood on one foot, and with the other kicked up their dresses behind, while talking to gentlemen. This fashion began with a celebrated beauty who "dared do any thing." Luckily, these "whims and oddities" are always of short duration, and are never adopted by young ladies of good taste and refinement.

Do not nod your head, or beat time with fan or foot while listening to music.

Never at a party consent to accompany another lady in a duet, unless you are accustomed to singing with her. Still worse—do not volunteer to "assist" her in a song that is not a duet. Each voice will interrupt and spoil the other. A lady who sings by ear only, cannot accompany one that sings by note.

One of the most horrible sounds imaginable is that produced by several fine voices all singing different songs. This cats' concert (as school-girls call it) results in a shocking and yet ludicrous discord, equally frightful and laughable. And yet all the performers are singing individually well. Try it.

EVER SOFT, GENTLE AND LOW

Talking so loudly that you can be heard all over the room. Or so low that you cannot be heard at all, even by those who are conversing with you. This last fault is the worst. To talk with one who has a habit of muttering unintelligibly, is like trying to read a letter illegibly written.

Using too often the word "madam" or "ma'am," which in fact, is now nearly obsolete in familiar conversation. In the old French tragedies the lovers addressed their mistresses as "madam." But then the stage Alexander wore a powdered wig, and a laced coat, knee-breeches, and a long-skirted waistcoat; and Roxana figured in a hoop-petticoat, a brocade gown, a flowered apron, and a towering gauze cap. The frequent use of "sir" is also out of fashion. "Yes, ma'am," "No, ma'am," "Yes, sir," "No, sir," no longer sounds well, except from children to their elders. If you have not distinctly heard what another lady has just said to you, do not denote it by saying, "Ma'am?" but remark to her, "Excuse me, I did not exactly hear you!"

Never, in a public parlour, place yourself in a position where you can secretly hear conversation that is not intended for you—for instance in a corner behind a pillar. If you hear yourself talked of, it is mean to stay and listen. It is a true adage that "Listeners seldom hear any good of themselves."

However smart and witty you may be considered, do not exercise your wit in rallying and bantering your friends. If you do so, their friendship will soon be worn out, or converted into positive enmity. A jest that carries a sting with it can never give a pleasant sensation to the object. The bite of a musquito is a very little thing, but it leaves pain and inflammation behind it, and the more it is rubbed the longer it rankles in the blood. No one likes to have their foibles or mishaps turned into ridicule—before other persons especially. And few can cordially join in a laugh that is raised against themselves.

The slightest jest on the personal defects of those you are conversing with, is an enormity of rudeness and vulgarity. It is, in fact, a sneer at the Creator that made them so. No human creature is accountable for being too small, or too large; for an ill-formed figure, or for ill-shaped limbs; for irregular features, or a bad complexion.

YOU ARE NEVER TOO OLD

Still worse, to rally any person (especially a woman) on her age, or to ask indirect questions with a view of discovering what her age really is. If we continue to live, we must continue to grow old. We must either advance in age, or we must die. Where then is the shame of surviving our youth? And when youth departs, beauty goes along with it. At least as much beauty as depends on complexion, hair, and teeth. In arriving at middle age, (or a little beyond it,) a lady must compound for the loss of either face or figure. About that period she generally becomes thinner, or fatter. If thin, her features shrink, and her skin shrivels and fades; even though she retains a slender and perhaps a girlish form. If she grows fat, her skin may continue smooth, and her complexion fine, and her neck and arms may be rounder and handsomer than in girlhood; but then symmetry of shape will cease—and she must reconcile herself to the change as best she can. But a woman with a good mind, a good heart, and a good temper, can never at any age grow ugly—for an intelligent and pleasant expression is in itself beauty, and the best sort of beauty.

The woman that knows how to grow old gracefully, will adapt her dress to her figure and her age, and wear colours that suit her present complexion. If her neck and arms are thin, she will not expose them under any circumstances. If her hair is grey, she will not decorate it with flowers and flimsy ribbons. If her cheeks are hollow, she will not make her face look still longer and thinner by shadowing it with long ringlets; and setting her head-dress far back—but she will give it as much softness as she can, by a light cap-border tied under her chin. She will not squeeze herself out of all human shape by affecting a long tight *corsage*; and she will wear no dresses glaring with huge flowers, or loaded with gaudy trimmings. She will allude to her age as a thing of course; she will speak without hesitation of former times, though the recollection proves her to be really old. She will be kind and indulgent to the young; and the young will respect and love her, and gladly assemble near her chair, and be amused and unconsciously instructed. As long as she lives and retains her faculties she will endeavour to improve, and to become still a wiser and a better woman; never excusing herself by indolently and obstinately averring that "she is too old to learn," or that she cannot give up her old-fashioned habits. If she finds that those habits are unwarrantable, or that they are annoying to her friends, she ought to relinquish them. No one with a mind unimpaired, and a heart still fresh, is too old to learn.

This book is addressed chiefly to the young; but we shall be much gratified by finding that even old ladies have found in it some advantageous suggestions on points that had hitherto escaped their notice.